CONCILIUM

THEOLOGY IN THE AGE OF RENEWAL

CONCILIUM

CONCILIUM/VOL. 33

PASTORAL THEOLOGY

THE RENEWAL
OF PREACHING
THEORY AND PRACTICE

edited by KARL RAHNER, S.J.

VOLUME 33

CONCILIUM
theology in the age of renewal

PAULIST PRESS
NEW YORK, N.Y. / GLEN ROCK, N.J.

Library of Congress Catalogue Card Number: 68-22795

Suggested Decimal Classification: 260

Paulist Press assumes responsibility for the accuracy of the English translations in this Volume.

PAULIST PRESS
EXECUTIVE OFFICES: 304 W. 58th Street, New York, N.Y. and 21 Harristown Road, Glen Rock, N.J.
Executive Publisher: John A. Carr, C.S.P.
Executive Manager: Alvin A. Illig, C.S.P.
Asst. Executive Manager: Thomas E. Comber, C.S.P.

EDITORIAL OFFICES: 304 W. 58th Street, New York, N.Y.
Editor: Kevin A. Lynch, C.S.P.
Managing Editor: Urban P. Intondi

Printed and bound in the United States of America by
The Colonial Press Inc., Clinton, Mass.

CONTENTS

vii

PART II

BIBLIOGRAPHICAL SURVEY

PART III

DOCUMENTATION CONCILIUM
Office of the Executive Secretary
Nijmegen, Netherlands

PREFACE

Karl Rahner, S.J./*Münster, W. Germany*

From its inception *Concilium* has deliberately set out to tackle burning questions in both the teaching and the practice of the Church today. Without doubt one of these burning questions concerns what is termed "the trouble with preaching". Preachers and congregations are fully aware of the difficulties designated by that expression. Many leave the Church because the language flowing from the pulpit has no meaning for them; it has no connection with their own life and simply bypasses many threatening and unavoidable issues. In fact, the sermon has often been characterized by dogmatizing, by boasting of formal and doctrinaire authority, by moralizing that was frequently arrogant and appeared pharisaical, and by a shunning of daily political or cultural problems which directly affected the Church.

This at least was the impression given to many members of the congregation. It is therefore not astonishing that as the preacher ascends into the pulpit, he is rather nervous, shy and uncertain of himself. In view of the growing weight of his daily pastoral tasks, the increasingly critical attitude of his audience, the problems created by the development of modern science for scriptural explanation and the growing complications of life in today's society at large, "the trouble with preaching" is becoming even more troublesome. It has become frighteningly

1

obvious that the priest's training in the art of preaching has for a long time been extraordinarily scanty. In most cases the whole of this training for preaching consisted in a mainly useless training for rhetoric and the use of the voice, some formal criteria and a summary of the history of preaching.

If this so-called pastoral technique meant very little in the *ensemble* of the various theological disciplines, the teachers of the key disciplines were equally little concerned about the Church's mission to preach. The particular art of translating theological insights into the language of preaching was left to the fitness or unfitness of the individual priest or was contorted by being forced into the harness of some formal laws of some peculiar rhetoric. Some changes have taken place as a result of the various attempts to revitalize the sermon, but, as the Bibliographical Survey of this volume indicates, these changes have resulted in little real progress or have already proceeded in directions which must be evaluated. Frequently a priest will use a merely superficial, modern, secular or theological jargon in the hope of coming a little closer to the audience, but ultimately this only reveals his helplessness and resignation with regard to the real task, the deeper task.

Granting the praiseworthy attempts to give the homily its own place and function in the celebration of the eucharist, the honest observer of the situation must admit that these experiments are not without difficulties of their own. The scriptural text too often serves merely as a springboard, and after a few introductory words something totally different is dealt with; the sermon dwindles into an exegetical or theological address or avoids precisely those questions which the Scripture passage threw up. If the homily is limited too exclusively to being just a sermon, we shall have a certain, not unproblematical, choice of topics, and if we renounce explicitly all dogmatic, moral or liturgical subjects, we can but impoverish the content of the sermon.

If one listens to a sermon in our churches on a feast day (Christmas, Easter, etc.), one realizes that a reform, based on exegesis alone, will not solve the difficulties. Moreover, the introduction of the vernacular into the liturgy has underlined the poverty of our sermons, since the growing familiarity with the direct text of the scriptures now really shows how alien and perplexed our understanding is with regard to these texts. It would be an ultimate capitulation if, in our wish to take Christianity seriously, we would shy away from the central truths of our faith and take refuge in a constant preaching about brotherly love, Christian political commitment, etc. All this is, no doubt, also centrally important and can provide the decisive key for the building up of a modern sermon, but in truth the actual proclamation then remains abstract and alien to life because it does not draw its strength from the heart of the Christian faith. The Christian who truly lives on the sources of faith, hope and charity, and who today particularly struggles to preserve his integrity, his strength to live and the power to exercise his mission, would then really have the impression that he has been left in the lurch by the preacher in matters that are decisive.

This volume has been conceived in the light of this way of understanding the present difficulties in preaching and the Church's mission to proclaim. According to the general character of *Concilium* and the specific purpose of the pastoral volumes in particular, this volume hopes to offer some practical help, although this should not be taken as a ready-made recipe. It was therefore necessary to include some difficult and not always easily digestible scientific treatment. We can only hope to bring about a fruitful reform if we attack the evil at the root, and it will cause no surprise that this means a return to the sources of our faith.

The biblical-theological contribution tries to clarify the notion of "Word of God" and shows how all preaching must go back to Jesus Christ himself, his Word and his Church. This brings out at the same time the kind of qualities that a "good" preacher should have. Two articles deal with the dogmatic aspects. Then an attempt is made to give some solution for the whole series of problems created by the slogan of "demythologization". One article shows the many levels of the reality of salvation and how this must be considered in a proper and differentiated way in the preparation and delivery of the sermon; another tries to throw some light on the relation between Word and sacrament. The theological preoccupations of recent years, the requirements laid down by Vatican Council II and above all the problems of the Latin American continent in matters of sacramental practice demanded a thorough treatment of this question.

Since the "moral sermon" in the best sense of the word is now a rarity, a well-known moral theologian was asked to give his views on this subject. In order to avoid an altogether too naive view of the practical methods, the acceptance and the intelligibility of the sermon, a sociologist who is also a theologian was invited to examine the psychological and sociological structures of preaching. Such investigations are the more instructive since they show how closely the sermon is connected with other forms of pastoral work. A radio producer reports on his work and his experiences in the field of preaching before the microphone. This is a very concrete complement to the previous contribution since it provides us with the critical reaction of the listener to a proclamation of the Word which is sober, unprejudiced, technically transmitted and thus "secularized", and this points out the responsibility and opportunities of the sermon. Here we can see how far in practice our preaching is out of touch with the expectations and feelings of modern man. Two shorter articles deal with two important specific questions. A well-known Evangelical theologian outlines the context, contained in man's experience, in which realities such as "salvation", "redemption" and "reconciliation" can be made intelligible without any diminution of their theological meaning. A South American theologian gives a clear and concise answer to the question whether lay preaching is not inevitable today in given circumstances.

In this volume it was planned to have two major sections in the Bibliographical Survey. Volume 20 of *Concilium* (*The Dynamism of Biblical Tradition*) devoted the Bibliographical

Survey section (pp. 117–158) to the topic of the sermon, to which we refer the reader here. In this volume the Bibliographical Survey investigates by what means preaching is helped in individual countries and what is being done to solve the difficulties of preaching by means of institutions, congresses and periodicals. The introduction attempts a summing up of our research. In the second article we intended to discover, with the help of professional collaborators, how far and by what means the Christian proclamation by radio or television can be successful. A survey of the totally different situations in the various countries might have produced valuable suggestions. In spite of much time and effort, it was not possible to collect sufficient material within the time that was available. Therefore, an accurate report had to be postponed, but it seemed nevertheless important in view of the difficulties to make the reader aware of the actuality of this task, and this is done at the close of the section.

Unfortunately, only a few questions could be singled out here. Thus, for instance, a long-planned contribution on the use and possibilities of the "occasional" sermon (at a funeral, baptism or wedding, etc.) has not been included. It would have been valuable to have a Protestant contribution on the attempts made, from the institutional and literary aspects, to improve the sermon. However, if one reads in the present volume about the data produced by the inquiry into modern means of helping the preacher, he will find that, in spite of the gaps and the provisional character of the points made herein, some sound indications are given, although they cannot pretend to be more than that.

PART I
ARTICLES

Heinrich Schlier/*Bonn, W. Germany*

The Chief Features of a New Testament Theology of the Word of God

The basis of all speaking about the Word of God in the New Testament is the datum that God himself became "flesh" in his Word (Jn. 1, 1f. 14). God "expressed" himself (Jn. 1, 18) in the Logos that "became flesh", that is, in Jesus of Nazareth. God expressed himself definitively in the person and history of Jesus. It was with Jesus that the Word, to which creation is indebted, entered history and it was with him that the Word of God's covenant with Israel was fulfilled in history (2 Cor. 1, 19f.). The event of God's Word took place in him.

I

JESUS CHRIST AS THE DEFINITIVE WORD OF GOD

This idea, which is not really thought out, but is certainly clearly expressed in John's gospel, can also be found elsewhere in the New Testament. Hebrews 1, 1f., for example, refers to God's "speaking" to us "by a Son" as his one and last speaking "in these last days", contrasting this with his many and various—and provisional—ways of speaking by the prophets "of old". God's speaking is thus concentrated in his definitive Word in the "Son". The passage in Acts 10, 36f., in which we are told that

God sent "the Word" (τὸν λόγον) to the sons of Israel and thus proclaimed peace by Jesus Christ, is also relevant here. This "Word" is the fulfillment of the Word "which occurred throughout all Judea". Here, as in the case of the usual translation of *dābhār* in the Septuagint, the concept ῥῆμα means the event seen in this perspective, taking place and at the same time expressing itself and addressing men. The Word, which God sent to the sons of Israel, is therefore the saving event, Jesus Christ, in Judea; this event is then summarized kerygmatically in the verses that follow—the history of Jesus Christ from the baptism of John up to the death on the cross and the resurrection of the Christ whom God appointed to be the judge of the living and the dead.

The apostle Paul also touches upon this datum—Jesus Christ is the Word of God, insofar as the Christ who entered into the kerygma and is proclaimed in it is the "Amen" pronounced by God on all his promises (2 Cor. 1, 19f.). In the Apocalypse, moreover, Christ is called "the Amen" (Apoc. 3, 14), and Chapter 19 states that the incomprehensible name of the future victor and judge is "the Word of God" (ὁ λόγος τοῦ θεοῦ).

II

The Relationship between the Apostolic Proclamation and Jesus as the Word of God

In the New Testament, however, what is meant by the Word of God is also and above all (and also partly terminologically) the apostolic proclamation—that is, what is known as the Gospel (of God or of Christ), the witness (of Christ), the kerygma; in some cases it is also known as the teaching, even what Jesus himself made known, according to Luke 5, 1; 8, 11. 21; 11, 28. What is the relationship between this Word and the Word of God that was Jesus himself? The statement in Romans 10, 17, which is by no means unequivocal and in which we are told that "faith comes from what is heard" and "what is heard comes by the event

(= word, ῥῆμα) of Christ", does perhaps indicate that there is a relationship. The event of Christ thus sets forth what is heard, what is given to us to hear, and this in turn leads to faith. But how does this come about? An answer to this question can be provided on the basis of statements in Paul's letters and in the gospels of John and Luke.

III

PAUL: THE REVELATION OF THE EXALTED LORD

To substantiate his argument that the Gospel is not the word of man, but the Word of God, the apostle Paul refers to the "revelation of Jesus Christ"—that is, to the direct disclosure of the exalted Christ which was granted to him, a disclosure which was an anticipation of the eschatological revelation. This "disclosure" is at the same time an illumination of his Word to the Gospel. God chose Paul and revealed the exalted Christ to him directly in this way, so that Paul would be able to let him speak in his Word (Gal. 1, 11ff.; 2 Cor. 4, 6). The Word of God in the sense of Gospel is, by virtue of its essential source, the legacy of the illuminating self-revelation of Jesus Christ in the apostolic Word, from which the "insight into the mystery of Christ" (Eph. 3, 4) speaks.

IV

JOHN'S GOSPEL: THE CALLING TO MIND OF THE SPIRIT

In the fourth gospel, Jesus, absorbed in the glory (δόξα) of the original Word of God's love (Jn. 17, 5. 24), is discussed openly as regards his way and his work in relation to the "Spirit". In the perspective of John's gospel, this is clearly seen in the words "He [the Spirit] will bear witness to me" (Jn. 15, 26) and "Whatever he [the Spirit] hears, he will speak" (Jn. 16, 13). Even more significant is the thought: "He [the Spirit] will bring to your re-

membrance all that I have said to you" (John 14. 26). "Calling
to mind" (ὑπομιμνῄσκειν) in connection with the "Spirit" has a
threefold meaning—to make present, to set out in exposition and
to allow to be experienced. The Spirit, who is the Spirit of the
Father and of Jesus, enables the person and the work of Jesus
to become present in such a way in his exposition that we experience him in his truth. He thus leads us "into all truth" by
allowing Jesus' δόξα to appear (Jn. 16, 13) and shows himself to
be the "Spirit of truth", the unveiled, valid reality (see Jn. 14,
17; 15, 26; 16, 13).

This Spirit, however, this disclosing power of the self-revelation of God and of Jesus Christ, speaks in the words of the
apostles of whom he has taken possession: "When the Counsellor
comes, whom I shall send to you from the Father, even the Spirit
of truth, who proceeds from the Father, he will bear witness to
me; and you also are witnesses, because you have been with me
from the beginning" (Jn. 15, 26–27). Not only the Spirit but
also the apostles are, according to John, witnesses to Jesus. They
do not, of course, bear witness to Jesus alongside each other, but
in such a way that the apostles proclaim Jesus in his truth through
the Spirit and the Spirit proclaims Jesus through them. The apostles' word thus continues Jesus' Word, which is God's Word (Jn.
15, 20; 17, 20).

John's understanding of the essence of the apostolic word as
the Word of the Spirit and Paul's understanding of the apostolic
word as the Word of revelation are not, however, mutually exclusive. On the one hand, the Spirit did not come to us, according
to John's gospel, until Jesus had been glorified (Jn. 7, 39; 16, 7),
and it was Jesus, hastening to his exaltation and later appearing
as the risen Lord, who granted the Spirit to us for the first time
(Jn. 20, 19ff.)—Easter and Pentecost occurring, in John, at the
same time. On the other hand, the Gospel is established, according to Paul, on the basis of Christ's revelation in the power of the
Spirit, who is, according to Paul, the Spirit in whom God himself
and Christ are disclosed (1 Cor. 2, 10ff.; Rom. 8, 9ff.). Christ
himself says that the Word, by which he has revealed himself,

comes through the power of his Spirit, and it is in this way that God is experienced by man (Rom. 8, 2; 1 Cor. 2, 13; 2 Cor. 11, 4; Eph. 6, 17).

V

LUKE: SEEING AND HEARING THE RISEN CHRIST

It is also possible to refer to the Acts of the Apostles in this connection. The "Word of God" is firmly established terminologically in Acts and has its very secure origin in the appearance of the risen Lord to the chosen witnesses (Acts 10, 40f.; see also 1, 3; 3, 15; 5, 32; 13, 31, etc.). These witnesses were to testify to what they had "seen and heard" (Acts 1, 8. 22; 2, 32), and for this purpose they were commissioned by the risen Lord and given their ministry (Acts 1, 2; 20, 24; see also 1, 17. 25). The one who disclosed the risen Lord—in other words, Jesus in his whole history—and gave the apostles words to speak about him was the "Holy Spirit". This illuminating "power" ($\delta\acute{v}v\alpha\mu\iota\varsigma$) was assigned to them as the gift of the exalted Christ, as the language of salvation opening the mouths and hearts of all (Acts 1, 8; 2, 4. 17ff. 33ff.; 4, 31; 5, 32; 10, 44ff., etc.). The Word of God, proclaimed by the Paul of the Acts, also has its origin in this seeing and hearing. This emerges clearly from Acts 9, 22. 26. It was, however, the exalted Kyrios who let himself be seen and heard in his heavenly light and made the will of God known in himself to Paul in the Acts of the Apostles, so that Paul, as the witness sent by him to the Gentiles and as the servant of his appearance in the power of the Spirit, would proclaim him as the Son of God for the conversion and the salvation of all men.

VI

THE WORD OF GOD IN THE WORD OF MEN
AND THE WORD OF MEN AS THE WORD OF GOD

In this way, God's Word is always the Word of God in the word of men, and the word of men as the Word of God is, in the historical sense, the Word of God. This is implied in Luke 10, 16: "He who hears you hears me." It is also clear in Acts that, on the one hand, it is God who proclaims (Acts 17, 30) or the risen Lord (Acts 26, 23) and that, on the other hand, God's Word is spoken "by the mouth" of the apostles (Acts 15, 7), by "God's servants" (Acts 4, 29), by Peter and John (Acts 8, 25), by Paul (Acts 17, 13; 18, 5. 11) and by Paul and Barnabas (Acts 13, 5. 46; 14, 25; 15, 36). This datum is formulated most clearly by Paul himself, who calls the Gospel of God or of Christ "my" or "our" Gospel (Rom. 2, 6; 16, 25; 1 Cor. 4, 3; Gal. 1, 11; 2, 2; 1 Thess. 1, 5. 8; 2 Thess. 2, 14; 2 Tim. 2, 8). In 1 Thessalonians 2, 13, he tells the Christians in Thessalonica that he thanks God without ceasing "that, when you received the Word of God which you heard from us (λόγον ἀκοῆς παρ' ἡμῶν τοῦ θεοῦ), you accepted it not as the word of men (λόγον ἀνθρώπων), but as what it really is, the Word of God (λόγον θεοῦ) which is at work in you believers". The Word of God is concealed in the word of men, but faith hears it and accepts it for what it is in truth. God preaches "through us" (2 Cor. 5, 20; Rom. 15, 18).

VII

THE ORIGINAL POWER OF GOD'S WORD

"Official" Mission and Surrender in Ministry and Witness

In this connection, two things should be borne in mind. The first is that mission and ministry are closely connected with this Word of God in its very origin. It is not a word suspended in a vacuum. Despite the fact that he also recognizes a charismatic word, Paul certainly accepts unequivocally the fact that "grace" (which is effective in the Gospel) and "apostleship" (ἀποστολή) are received directly from Christ and belong together (Rom. 1, 5), just as he accepts God's establishment of the "Word of reconciliation" together with the "ministry of reconciliation" (2 Cor. 5, 18f.). If God's Word has, in its origin, a kind of "official" character—Paul refers to his οἰκονομία (1 Cor. 9, 17; see also 4,

1f.)—then it only emerges as the Word of God by its bearer, the apostle, placing himself personally entirely at its disposal. God's Word is, in a certain sense, dependent on the one who carries it, and is at the same time also above him (1 Cor. 14, 36; Phil. 1, 12; 4, 15; 1 Thess. 1, 5, etc.). According to Acts 20, 32, Paul commends the assembled elders "to God and to the Word of his grace" (see also Acts 6, 7; 11, 1; 12, 24, etc.).

God's Word therefore takes the one who proclaims it into its ministry. Paul himself is "the minister of the Gospel" (Col. 1, 23; Eph. 3, 7; 1 Cor. 4, 1; see also Lk. 1, 2; Acts 6, 2. 4; 1 Tim. 1, 12). What is more, personal surrender to the Gospel, a surrender which discloses and at the same time keeps the Gospel free, is above all required in this ministry of the Gospel. The apostle may not allow his own self-seeking to stand in the way of this ministry, either by claiming any need to maintain his own life or by any impure motives in the proclamation of the Gospel (1 Cor. 9, 1; 1 Thess. 2; 2 Cor. 4, 1ff.) or by making light of human wisdom (1 Cor. 2, 1ff.) or with any spiritual experience which may conceal the Gospel (2 Cor. 11, 23ff.; 12, 1ff.). The apostle is bound not only to bring about a holy change "in the spirit of faith" in which he speaks (2 Cor. 1, 12; 4, 2) or to practice asceticism for the sake of the Gospel (1 Cor. 9, 27ff.), but also to suffer for the Word and in this way to testify to the sufferings of Christ (2 Cor. 1, 3ff.; 4, 6; 11, 23ff.; 12, 7). The ministry of the Word has been fulfilled when the apostle's change has itself become a witness and he can say: "What you have learned and received and heard and seen in me, do" (Phil. 4, 9).

The Presence of Salvation in God's Word

It is through this Word, God's Word in the word of men, that the one who speaks in it through men is made present to men. It is in this Word that his salvation comes to meet men, his salvation which is at the same time their salvation. Such un-Greek expressions as καίαγγέλλειν κηρύσσειν τὸν χριστὸν (Phil. 1, 17; 1 Cor. 1, 23; 2 Cor. 1, 19; Col. 1, 28, etc.) mean not only that Christ is proclaimed, but also that he is made present in this proclamation (1 Cor. 11, 26). Reconciliation is offered from God in the "Word of reconciliation" (2 Cor. 5, 19f.). When Paul "imparts wisdom" (σοφίαν λαλεῖ: 1 Cor. 2, 6), this wisdom, which is Christ, is brought to light in what is spoken. When "the righteousness of God is revealed" in the Gospel (Rom. 1, 17), this means—as the antithesis (Rom. 1, 18) shows—their mutual efficacy.

According to 2 Corinthians 4, 2, the Gospel is a φανέρωσις ἀληθείας, an allowing of the truth to appear. Paul expresses this idea most strikingly in 2 Timothy 1, 10f., where he says that Christ himself has allowed "life and immortality to be brought to light" in the fulfillment of the apostolic Gospel. This means that the Gospel is also a δύναμις, a power of God for salvation (Rom. 1, 16; 1 Cor. 1, 18). As such, it is experienced in faith and thus in hearing and accepting obedience (Rom. 10, 16; 2 Cor. 9, 13). To those who refuse it or are "disobedient" to it, it shows its critical power (Heb. 4, 12f.) in the absence of salvation and the presence of disaster (Rom. 11, 28ff.; 1 Cor. 1, 18ff.; 2 Cor. 4, 3ff.; 2 Thess. 1, 8). The divine intention of the Gospel is directed toward bringing about, in and with Christ, justice, reconciliation, truth, salvation, life, peace and freedom—in a word, grace (2 Cor. 4, 10ff.; 1 Cor. 7, 15. 22. 25; Gal. 1, 6; 5, 13; Eph. 4, 4; Phil. 2, 16; Col. 1, 6. 23. 27; 1 Tim. 6, 12, etc.); it is the establishment of a new covenant (καινὴ διαθήκη: 2 Cor. 3, 6), the gathering together of those who are attracted by and endowed with such eschatological possessions as God's "called" and "holy" people, the building up of the οἰκοδομή of the body of Christ in the Church (1 Cor. 3, 9; 14, 3ff.; 2 Cor. 10, 8; 12, 19; Eph. 4, 12. 16) and, in all this, making visible and discernible the manifold wisdom of God (Eph. 3, 8ff.). It therefore redeems the promises of God's Word made to the patriarchs, the promises which were "confirmed" by Christ (Rom. 15, 8; see also 2 Cor. 1, 20).

In the apostolic word, God's Word has become, through Christ, definitive, and as such determines the present eschatological time: "Behold, now is the acceptable time; behold, now is the day of salvation" (2 Cor. 6, 1f.). Now is the time, since the fragrance of the knowledge of Christ, an aroma from death to death and an aroma from life to life, has spread, through the preaching of the apostle, throughout the earth (2 Cor. 2, 14ff.) and "the new creation" has come about (2 Cor. 5, 17).

VIII

DEVELOPMENT AND EXPOSITION OF THE APOSTOLIC WORD
IN THE PROCLAMATION OF THE CHURCH

This brings us to one final consideration. God's Word in the apostolic word has not only been established and preserved in various ways—in homologetical, catechetical, liturgical and juridical traditions and finally in "Scripture"—in the Church, the people called forth by this Word. This Word is also and above all, while determining this event and being determined by it, perpetuated in the continuing proclamation of the Church.

The Fact and the Manner of Transmitting the Word

The fact itself appears in the letters of Paul. He says of his "fellow workers" or collaborators that they have devoted themselves to "the work of the Lord" and calls them "God's collaborators in the Gospel" (1 Cor. 16, 10; 1 Thess. 3, 2; see also 2 Cor. 1, 19; 8, 23; Phil. 2, 22; Eph. 6, 22, etc.). It is, of course, also possible to extend this idea to all those who, like Stephen and Philip in the Acts of the Apostles, are called εὐαγγελιζόμενοι τὸν λόγον (Acts 6, 8ff.; 8, 4ff.) or to the bishops, priests, elders and overseers who appear in Acts or in Paul's pastoral letters. Furthermore, it should also be borne in mind that the members of the various communities—and this applies above all to the charismatics—are called upon to "build each other up" or to "encourage each other" (1 Thess. 5, 11; 2 Thess. 3, 15; Heb. 3, 13; 10, 25, etc.; see also Rom. 15, 14; 1 Cor. 14, 1ff. 26ff.).

The question remains, however, as to the manner in which their proclamation continues that of the apostles and thus that of the Word of God. We can point to the following places in

Paul's letters. The apostle's collaborators have, as 1 Corinthians
4, 17 shows, the task of "reminding" the members of the various
communities "of my [the apostle's] ways in Christ, as I teach
them everywhere in the Church". Like the charismas generally
in the community, the charismas of the "Word" also catch fire on
the basis of "the testimony of Christ" which "was confirmed
among you"—that is, by the apostle (1 Cor. 1, 6f.). And when
Paul calls upon the Christians in Thessalonica to "comfort one
another" (παρακαλεῖν), he urges them to do so "with these [that
is, his own] words" (which he has just written to them) (1 Thess.
4, 18; see also 1 Cor. 11, 2).

What, then, is expressed in the word of the collaborators and
the members of the communities is the "remembered" apostolic
word that is accepted as binding and is passed on, insofar as it
is not simply recapitulated, but is also independently expounded
and developed. As such it is also God's Word, insofar as it allows
the apostolic word to speak. In this sense, it is a derived Word
of God, because it no longer has its origin in the direct self-dis-
closure of Jesus Christ in the Word (the Gospel)—by virtue of
the Spirit who reveals him as the risen and exalted Lord and
allows him to be experienced as such—but in the apostolic word
and, only through this, in revelation. Revelation itself is closed
and unrepeatable (1 Cor. 3, 10f.; 15, 8ff.; Eph. 2, 20). This
certainly does not mean that Jesus Christ is no longer able to
be present in the Word. However, it does mean that he can only
be so insofar as the word of the apostles' successors allows the
apostolic word itself and, in this word, God's Word to speak.

The Conditions of True Continuation

The later pastoral letters are especially concerned with this
problem of the continuation of God's Word. Timothy is admonished to "command and teach these things" (1 Tim. 4, 11;
see also 5, 7; 6, 3), to "remind them of this" (2 Tim. 2, 14; 3,
1; see also Tit. 2, 1; 3, 8, etc.). On the one hand, this "calling
to mind" means that the disciple and successor should receive
and hand on the apostolic word and no other (1 Tim. 4, 16; 6,

14. 20). On the other hand, however, it also means that he should not repeat it mechanically, but develop it with understanding in the concrete situation. In order to do this, it is necessary for him to be "nourished on the words of the faith and of the good doctrine which he has followed" (1 Tim. 4, 6) and to allow himself to be granted understanding in everything by the Lord (2 Tim. 2, 7). For this result to be achieved, he must be aroused by the Spirit who has virtually been communicated to him (1 Tim. 4, 14; 2 Tim. 1, 6f. 14), and his life must be a concrete imitation of Jesus Christ and of the apostle (1 Tim. 1, 18ff.; 4, 14; 6, 11ff.; 2 Tim. 3, 10, etc.).

The continuation of God's Word in the proclamation of the Church is therefore dependent on the firm foundation of the Word of revelation, a Word that must be expressed and made intelligible in the power of the Spirit and be made present by personal surrender in its openness as the Word of God. Thus the ministry of the Word fits in with the total ministry of the Church: "As each has received a gift, employ it for one another, as good stewards of God's varied grace; whoever speaks, as one who utters oracles of God; whoever renders service, as one who renders it by the strength which God supplies; in order that in everything God may be glorified through Jesus Christ. . . ." (1 Pet. 4, 10f.).[1]

[1] For further reading on this subject, cf. R. Asting, *Die Verkündigung des wort Gottes im Urchristentum. Dargestellt an den Begriffen "Wort Gottes", "Evangelium" und "Zeugnis"* (Stuttgart, 1939); K. H. Schelkle, "Das Wort Gottes in der Kirche," in *ThQ* 133 (1953), pp. 278–93; R. Bultmann, "Der Begriff des Wort Gottes im Neuen Testament," in *Glauben und Verstehen* I (Tübingen, ²1954), pp. 268–93; G. Bornkamm, "Gotteswort und Menschewort im Neuen Testament," in *Kirche und Zeit* 12 (1957), pp. 301–5; idem, *Studien zu Antike und Christentum* (Munich, 1963), pp. 223–36; H. Schlier, *Wort Gottes* (Würzburg, ²1962); idem, "Wort II (Biblisch)," in *Handbuch theologischer Grundbegriffe* II (Munich, 1963), pp. 845–67; O. Semmelroth, *Wirkendes Wort. Zur Theologie der Verkündigung* (Frankfurt, 1962); L. Scheffczyk, *Von der Heilsmacht des Wortes* (Munich, 1966).

Karl Rahner, S.J./*Münster, W. Germany*

Demythologization and the Sermon

The word "demythologization" was coined by Rudolf Bultmann and his followers to mark their particular approach to biblical and theological hermeneutics. It has become a catchword, used for everything or nothing, and rather arbitrarily. In this article it is impossible to define this concept or to subject it to critical examination as it is used by Bultmann himself or by those theologians who are (or think they are) his disciples. Nor can I give here my own explanation of the term or lay down what is possibly meant by "myth" in Christian speech, let alone in the content of the Christian message. I am more concerned with pastoral theology here, and therefore neither will I examine the exact and difficult relation between speech and content, between what is said and what is meant, between image and concept, between expression and the presentation pattern used in the expression; all this concerns a relationship which is rather more complicated than may appear in what follows. But this need not affect the practical use of what I shall try to put forth here.

I

DEMYTHOLOGIZATION AS A METHOD OF "TRANSLATION"

1. *The Need for a Constantly New Explanation*

The word "demythologization" in the title is used here simply as a symbol for a very simple question: How should one preach in the present state of theology, and, above all, exegesis? I say "how", not "what", although these two aspects of preaching are closely connected, for it is clear that the content of the sermon can only be the message of the Gospel as understood by the Church, and nothing else. But this one and enduring content appears in Scripture (and of course also in tradition) clothed in the most varied concepts, and in all kinds of images, aspects and contexts. These concepts frequently have their own variegated history which is not an independent contribution by the Church. They are not equally intelligible to every age. What explains and what has to be explained, the doubtful and the obvious, are not the same in every age, and can even change places. The form of preaching in a particular age must be "translated" into another form of preaching to make the message understood, particularly if the meaning of the message must remain the same. This preservation of identity cannot be achieved by the mere repetition of old expressions if the mentality and concepts change in secular society through an historical development which is not under the Church's control. Often one has to start with the old expression of a theological statement and then return to it, but it has to be "translated" in the body of the sermon, and such a translation can, without becoming a message in its own right, form the main part or even the whole of a sermon if it is to be intelligible and credible.

2. Revelation in Secular Speech

The Church's language is not a language apart but is the language of the secular world in spite of being determined and shaped by the content of revelation. God's revelation uses human words that were already current and loaded with overtones from the surrounding world. These overtones are not simply eliminated because a given word is now used in a statement in the process of revelation. When this common speech undergoes alterations in sense, bearing and intelligibility, even when the words remain phonetically the same, then the language of the Church has to change accordingly. For instance, one can no longer use the word "transubstantiation" without further explanation in speaking of the eucharist, when the meaning of "substance" today is dominated by that given it in chemistry, for then it would certainly not express the change which takes place at consecration. Nor can one any longer talk glibly about three "Persons" in God (even though we maintain the formula), when modern man understands by "person" something which, if multiplied by three, would simply be heresy and not dogma.

That we, as clergy, often do not realize this comes from the fact that *we* (but not those that listen to us), like some other people, use several kinds of language (professional, common, etc.) and so do not notice it when we slip from one type of language into another, partially "translating" from one use into another. Gagarin, who was "up there" with his spaceship, really can only regard it as ridiculous nonsense when we talk about God "up there in heaven", until we have explained to him what we really mean. We should have "translated" on the spot. What must a modern medical doctor think when we talk about being redeemed by the "blood" of Jesus? It is bound to appear to him as an old-fashioned tale, a piece of mythology. He simply lacks the time we clergy have to learn the old religious language as well as his own. We must translate for him what we want to say, even though Scripture and tradition speak of Jesus' "blood". If there is time we can come back to the old formula in the sermon and tell him that this meant the same thing as what he was told before in "translation". What we mean by the "fire of hell" can just as well be said without the fire, and it would be wise for us to do so when our audience thinks of fire as a combustion process with oxygen and we have once again to explain laboriously that that is not what we mean. We cannot even take for granted, with Thomas Aquinas, that everyone knows what is meant by "God" and simply try to convince the listener that this "God" really exists.

3. *Modes of Speech and Intelligibility*

The question of "demythologization and the sermon", then, simply means for the preacher the question of what principles should guide him in the translation from the language of Scripture and tradition into a language that can be understood today. When and insofar as such a translation avoids mythical elements that are contained in the old words but not in what they are meant to express, we may call such a translation "demythologization". Basically this task is very complex; we have to carry over the enduring message from the language of one age to that of another age which in the world of today is undergoing profound and rapid change. I take for granted as understood that this problem is a permanent one and particularly urgent today, and I beg the reader to keep this in mind. He must realize that the language he in fact speaks, and in which he preaches, is a highly complex structure, never totally present in all its elements, never the same for any two people, and constantly changing. Everyone speaks a different mixture of common parlance, educated language, sociologically conditioned language, poetry and sacred language. All these modes of speech within one language constantly overlap. Everyone speaks and understands himself and others only in a common type of communication which, however, is far from homogeneous in itself, but pluralistic. No word can only mean one thing but fits into a vast texture of words, modified in every case, and the meaning comes only through within this context. Every word is wrapped in various associated meanings, feelings and experiences, and each word has its own peculiar connotation for every individual. All this changes constantly, and whether this is a slow or a fast process is secondary.

Here we should also remember that no "definition" of a word is final; one defines with other words which should be defined in turn. But definition is then no longer possible because one cannot go on indefinitely, and it is totally untrue that there are words which can be absolutely clear *in themselves* and need no further explanation. Therefore, we have to be reconciled to a language which is not subject to conscious control and, though apparently precise, is in reality obscure. We must rely on the way in which words are used in spite of their limitations.

II
GENERAL RULES FOR TRANSLATING THE MESSAGE IN THE SERMON

What has been said about language in general and many other things holds also for religious language. I take all this for granted here, as well as the fact that all religious speech in the Church of necessity is centered in the content of a transmitted message which is—or, to put it more cautiously, ought to be—translated into a message for today.

1. *Demand for Serious Theological Preparation*

First of all, such a "translation" demands of the preacher a serious theological preparation which must constantly be renewed. He should not think that he has prepared himself adequately during the perhaps lengthy period of his theological training. The dogmatic, moral and biblical theology of earlier days was already such a "translation"; that theology started from statements of the magisterium or those found in Scripture, and then proceeded to try to understand these statements and to express what they were meant to say. This necessarily postulated the use of other words, because an explanation and the thing to be explained cannot be expressed in the same words. In fact, these words which were used to explain were not yet available to the authority from which the statements originated, and therefore were taken from another kind of speech; in other words, there was "translation". But if the earlier theology was already a translation, this does not mean that it was so apt that a preacher can use it for what has to be said today. He has to develop his theology because he has to translate differently from twenty years ago, and this development must go on in theology itself. The preacher has to take note of that.

2. Hearing as the World Hears

The preacher must have an ear for the modes of speech and their nuances that are the context of his translation. This is not quite as obvious as it sounds. These modes of speech are not clearly and consciously distinguished; there exist no dictionaries for this use of speech, where one can look up what word belongs to what mode of speech and how one should translate a word from one mode to another. The preacher himself unconsciously mixes up these modes of speech and uses "alien" words without noticing it, words which will be understood wrongly or not at all. He may, for instance, speak in all simplicity about the "poor souls in purgatory" without realizing that "souls", "poor" and "purgatory" may mean nothing to his listener or be understood wrongly. He may talk about the "outpouring of sanctifying grace" without realizing that those words will be understood by his audience in *their* mode of speech and so usually misunderstood. He may use the term "original sin", unaware of the fact that this means something to the audience that does not in fact exist; such a term teaches them nothing and actually creates difficulties about the faith, while he has long forgotten the explanation of this obscure term in earlier days, if it was ever satisfactorily explained at all. We talk about "temporal punishment due to sin"; in the mind of the listener, this conjures up the picture of a few months in prison and makes him wonder whether such a situation really exists in afterlife. He might be better served by being presented the image of a painful neurosis he has brought upon himself through his own fault and the after-effects of which he has to bear with even after he has been freed from the guilt aspect. But how can an audience come to such an understanding when we talk about "temporal punishment" as if this were something obvious?

The preacher should be able to hear his own sermon with the ears of his actual audience. Then he will automatically begin to find out that he has to "translate" and the best way of translating. He must realize that, because of his training and clerical situation, he is talking in a religious and theological dialect from which only a few words have wandered into the speech of his audience. Of course, this does not mean that such a word will then pass from "being familiar" into "being really understood". We may use the words "the ascension of Jesus", and the words may be familiar to the listener, but whether he then understands them in their genuinely credible sense is a very different question.

3. *The Need for Self-Criticism*

The preacher must produce the *right kind* of translation. A translation could curtail or falsify the meaning of the words and so produce a "heretical" translation. This is the great danger in the question of demythologization. To control the correctness of such a translation is the function of theology at large and of the individual preacher, in humble contact with the Church's magisterium. This magisterium does not itself provide a ready-made translation into the language of modern man, but it has the duty to watch over this translating process. Such control can often take a long time before it is exercised and can be difficult. Think, for instance, of the controversy about whether and how "transubstantiation" could and should be translated to be intelligible today. Or think about the question of "original sin" when it is said to be "inherited from Adam through procreation". It is not so easy to say what is meant by "from Adam" (monogenism or not?), what is meant by "procreation" (certainly not simple and "normal" or even lustful copulation, since original sin is not bypassed by artificial insemination), or what is meant by "inherited" (we certainly do not inherit the *actual* sin of Adam). How then should we translate in such a way as to preserve the dogma and to eliminate views which are not dogma and not credible? The preacher must in any case be seriously self-critical about his "translation" and constantly check its correctness with regard to theology and the Church. He cannot make it easy for himself by simply repeating the formulae of the magisterium or the theology learned at the seminary and merely using a different style. This would certainly not ensure that these formulae would "reach" the listener and stir his faith, nor could the preacher be certain that, understood and interpreted according to the mode of speech of his audience, these formulae would not give rise to heresy rather than dogma.

4. *How Freely Should We Translate?*

Today a preacher will frequently have to preach in "translated" terms only. He may also often be required to use both the traditional terms and their translation. When, for instance, he has to explain a biblical text or to deal with a solemn declaration of the magisterium, he will have to use the old formulae of Scripture and tradition and show that he fully respects them even though he proceeds directly with an explanation and "translation" of them. On other occasions, he will only use the language of "translation" because time and spiritual ability are limited. The meaning of "treasury of the Church"—to give another illustration—is more easily and better put across to a large audience in a sermon by not using the expression at all; "communion with Christ and all those who are united in God's love" (which is, again, better than "with all saints") explains the real meaning more quickly and more intelligibly. This is, of course, different from its treatment at a high theological level, which has to take into account the history of dogma and ideas. The choice of method must be decided by the ecclesial and educational sense of the preacher.

5. *Should Theological Problems Be Discussed in the Pulpit?*

Proper theological controversies about the right kind of "translation" or "demythologization" should not be dealt with in the pulpit. This is not because the audience is thought to be lacking in intelligence and therefore should not be told about theological controversies, but because in the sermon from the pulpit (as distinct from a theological address) the Gospel should be proclaimed. The place for theological problems is elsewhere. The members of the congregation must be "edified"—i.e., confronted with God's claim on their life; God's grace should be offered to the faithful in the Word of the Gospel, which has its own effectiveness. That is the real purpose of a sermon. A theologically well-trained preacher has enough to preach about and can say all that is really important without indulging in such controversies. He can, for instance, preach the Easter event (even starting with the Gospel pericopes) in a "faithful" way without giving a learned exposé of what details in the narrative of the paschal apparitions belong to the historical experience of the disciples and what is the plastic and visual expression of their paschal faith. One can, in the same way, preach perfectly well about the proper theological significance of Jesus' baptism without having to discuss what the "form of a dove" could mean in the modern picture of the world and without giving the impression that we must cling to the physical reality of this dove to be orthodox. In such cases one should keep the scriptural statement within the unbroken unity of content and expression and interpret this whole in the light of the certain, real, religiously and existentially significant context without explicitly interpreting specific elements as *mere* "image" and presentation.

The preacher should know about such controversies and should preach in such a way that the critical consciousness of the truth is not upset, either in himself or in his listeners who are theologically informed. But these controversies are not, as such, a subject for a sermon. When the preacher knows that some listeners are genuinely troubled by such controversial issues, and that they will not be satisfied with his sermon or will be disturbed in their faith, he should certainly enlighten them, but in a theological lecture, not in his sermon. If the preacher is genuinely concerned about the reality of the Gospel and its "existential yet orthodox interpretation", and not about showing off his own theological knowledge and acumen, it should not be difficult for him to keep this rule. It will not always be easy to distinguish in a particular case between a correct translation of the Gospel in the pulpit and dealing with questions about what exactly the correct translation is, since sometimes the listeners can only be reached from the pulpit and one has to use the occasion in a kind of auxiliary way for plain theological instruction. If a preacher is in doubt about the adequate ("moral") certainty of a "translation", he should keep it to himself and simply say what he has to say in the traditional mode of speech. *Everyone* talks in a mixed mode of speech where the elements are *never* fully and consciously assimilated. It is therefore inevitable that a preacher will expect his listeners to be aware of some traditional religious language that has not yet been wholly "translated".

III

SPECIAL RULES FOR PREACHING EVENTS FROM SALVATION HISTORY

The general rules thus far indicated need some specification with the regard to the translation of events of *salvation history* reported in the sacred writings, events which must be transmitted and interpreted ("made actual") in our present mode of speech. This is the main point of the program of "demythologization".

1. *Events Should Not Be Reduced to Mere Conceptual or Existential Abstractions.*

Evidently, the preacher should not speak of these narratives of the events of salvation history in Scripture in such a way that all that remains of the true "meaning" is but an "idea", however "existentially" such an idea is understood and however much it is presupposed that it can only appeal to us through this "story" and precisely in this "story" (why?)—e.g., the story of Jesus' death on the cross. There is a history which has happened once-for-all and signifies *our* salvation as such. We remain bound to this history and it cannot be turned into a basically abstract idea through some "existential" interpretation. Man must work out his salvation within his history and not outside it. This history is always experienced as history; it refers through all human dimensions to the history of mankind as a whole and can only be understood in its frank acceptance. God works in and with this history, manifests his will through it, and what has happened once "here and now" can mean salvation for all. Such an historical event does not confront men from other ages as something that happened "once upon a time" and from "outside". What was "then" manifested as God's saving will and as an irrevocable fact in the eschatological history of Jesus is at work in God's grace as the ultimate ground and the ultimate moving force of the whole of history and therefore also at the root of all human existence. And so man meets his own "self" in an apparently alien history and discovers himself there.

Today, as in the past, the preacher must "proclaim" God's dealings with man in salvation history as real events and as salvation (somewhat like Paul in 1 Corinthians 15, 1). He should always and frankly "evoke" this history as a living presence so that modern man, with his rational, scientific, technological and therefore "unhistorical" mentality, can see that he is a man—i.e., an historical being—and that in this history he is confronted with what has always been operative in his innermost being and in grace. The proclamation must always unite the historical report, which is never mere neutral history, with the appeal to present existence.

2. *No Need To Be Archaic or To "Harmonize"*

The question still remains: How do we preach salvation history today? For us, today, it can no longer be a simple matter of recounting the reported events of salvation history exactly as they are put down in the Bible. We ourselves have to speak, and if *our* language is a mere repetition, we will give the impression that everything happened in *empirical history* precisely as we *recount* it. When, for instance, we recount Jesus' words, particularly as they appear in John, we should avoid the impression that they are a kind of tape recording of the words of the "historical" Jesus, with perhaps an abbreviation here and there. There is no need to labor so hard at harmonizing the Easter apparitions and to behave as if, historically, we knew more about them than Paul in 1 Corinthians 15 and as if we did not have to take into account that much in these narratives may well be a dramatic presentation of the simple fact of faith that Jesus has triumphed and is truly risen. We may simply accept the fact that the story of Jesus' childhood contains a piece of *midrash,* an illustrative explanation of the beginnings of the Messiah.

3. *The Combination of "Historical" Report and Theological Interpretation*

To return to matters of principle, we must also "translate"— i.e., "differentiate", in this case—when we ourselves preach about events of salvation history as reported in Scripture. It is not that we should deal with the *process* of this differentiation (to be developed later) in the pulpit. This would in most cases be a contradiction of the rule mentioned previously. But the preacher must know about this and use it when he himself does the proclaiming and does not merely read texts which do it for him. The scriptural narratives of salvation history form a unity, as has already been said. They unite the "historical" element with its interpretation in the proclamation of this historical element in depth. The earlier proclamation of those days brought the God-intended depths of salvation history to the surface of historical manifestation, at an empirical level where its experience was barely distinguishable from that of everyday life. It narrated this real history in a "simple" manner which proclaimed the "historical" event and its true interpretation (giving the real depth of this real event) in a unity which was not consciously worked out or seen. And so they made this deeper level of reality "visible". Thus there arose a "literary genre" in such reports of salvation history which is, of course, extraordinarily differentiated in itself and which is not easily and directly intelligible for us.[1] For this kind of reporting, miracles were correctly understood (I cannot deal here with their truth and validity) and at the same time interpreted as something "miraculous", as events at the same daily empirical level that was experienced as normal. The resurrection of Jesus was almost presented as an event which led Jesus back into the field of existence which he had left in truth and decisively by his death; Jesus himself appeared as a man who was credited—with a minimum of goodwill—straightaway with a heavenly origin.

4. *A Modified Way of Looking at the Event of Revelation*

It may astonish us, but it was not surprising in earlier ages that the post-apostolic experience of life provides practically no new examples for the pattern in which the earlier events of the old salvation history were presented. *We,* however, living in this present age, have to think and speak differently precisely in order to preserve what the old Christian faith saw and believed, though in a manner that was historically conditioned and more on the surface of history than in its depth. We have to see the nuances and speak accordingly. On the one hand—and this corresponds to our present total experience of existence— man exists in a "broken up" existence within the incomprehensibility of the absolute mystery that is called "God". Therefore, the data of the scientifically experimenting and critically verifying experiences of daily life are not, to start with, reality and history *tout court,* even though one may use the terms "history" and "historical" for this everyday experience by itself. On the other hand, man's divine (i.e., filled with God's sanctifying, forgiving and revealing self-communication) religious dimension in depth and his real history are not something totally divorced from his historical existence, hermetically sealed off as a kind of abstract "existence". On the contrary, this divine self-

---

[1] I have taken the liberty here to use, in a slightly altered form, some points I made in my essay "Der Glaube des Priesters heute" which has appeared recently in my book *Knechte Christi. Meditationen zum Priestertum* (Freiburg, 1967), pp. 13–44, esp. pp. 28f.

communication and the experience of it penetrate into the wide spaces of man's and the world's historical existence; they transform this existence, become manifest in it, interpret it and take shape in word, worship and religious community. Thus it comes into its own without, of course, ever completely identifying itself with these forms of objectivization in the dimension of daily experience.

Where such an objectivization succeeds genuinely and "cleanly", as in the people of Israel and its great believers, there we have salvation history in the full sense of the word. Where this self-promise of God becomes so manifest in the depth and continuity of history that one who is prepared to believe sees there something that is valid, unsurpassable, irreversible and ultimately credible for all men, there is Jesus crucified and risen, the Son of the Father in the straightforward sense, who alone achieved the total surrender to the will of God in the depth of his existence. That is why we must radically maintain here (though more consciously than in earlier times) the old dogma of Jesus' true humanity and leave salvation history up to Jesus in the unity *and* the difference of its dimensions. One should therefore not look for this divine identity wherever we have mainly elements of the secular and historical limitation and conditioning, human words and an historically conditioned mentality, which are all patterns of presentation and have their own right to exist. On the other hand, we must not separate and exclude this divine element from the *one* reality which also embraces daily experience. We must not deny it the right to be so manifest in this "empirical historicity" that "the eye of faith" can recognize these manifesting elements in "empirical" reality through the experience of grace and the acceptance of grace, whenever man is *willing* to see with this eye of faith.

5. *Understanding the Various Dimensions of the Realities of Salvation*

Modern theology is engaged in disentangling the various dimensions of this image of revealed salvation today insofar as this differs from the more simple image of earlier times. All the critical methods of theological, historical and (especially) biblical hermeneutics (e.g., the hermeneutics of *Formgeschichte*), basic theology and that history of dogma which is learning and teaching how to look at history—all these methods are but means to understand this multidimensional reality as such, at least insofar as these methods are relevant from the point of view of orthodoxy and kerygma. In this way these theologians must make clear that this reality, understood in these dimensions, was always there, even though an earlier, so to speak "two-dimensional", view could only see the depth of this reality when brought to the surface, and also emphasize that this depth vanishes completely with some modern critics who are no masters of their trade and can only see the immediate.

Therefore, modern theology is laboriously learning to distinguish, to see nuances, and a preacher should be aware of this, even when he stands in the pulpit and is not concerned with critical theology or exegesis as such. "Wonder" must be sharply distinguished from "miracle", and "hypostatic union" should not be a cover-up for latent monophysitism. The Son of God is not a God dressed up in a human uniform, but a real man, totally a creature of adoration and obedience, shaped by the environment, language and the theological thought of his time, burdened with the genuine human fate of darkness and death, but whose *ultimate* truth and reality is "radically" that of God himself. The descent of the Logos into the flesh must be seen as meaning for Jesus and for us in our experience of Jesus the ascent into the inscrutable mystery of God. Today we must pass again through the history of Christology in the New Testament, beginning with the situation before Paul, through Mark (including earlier traditions), and from Paul to John, and we cannot simply begin where Paul and John, each in his own way, left off. The real beginning lies in the history of the man Jesus, which for us *began* with the experience that here was a man like ourselves. Genuine divine revelation is not a matter of sentences communicated by heaven to "down below" by telephone, but the historical and concrete realization of God's self-communication at the root of man and his history, a history which is guided and achieved in and through God, the Lord himself.

6. This Change Involves a Slow and Uneven Process.

It is not astonishing that such a change in outlook needs time, varies from one to another, can lead to partial or total cases of blindness, and so makes one wonder whether all of us, who want to believe in the Church, still see the same thing. What I have said about the theological situation is no patent remedy to cope with any and all theological details. In many individual cases it will need labor and patience to find out what elements in a statement belong to the real meaning and what is simply the result of an "outlook". Very often no clear decision is possible. The modern theologian may run the risk of seeing, in a particular case, less than is actually there and was seen to be there in the old view. In general, however, it remains true that the difference between what is meant and what was said is realized more clearly and more consciously today than before. This holds not only for "transcendental" truths of the faith but also for the historical realities of our salvation history as expressed in the sources.

7. The Task of All Proclamation Remains the Same.

Although this statement looks like an exaggeration and is exposed to misunderstandings because of its briefness, it nevertheless has to be said if we want to make clear how the preacher of today must preach the earlier events of salvation honestly and credibly. At this point it is impossible to give more precise details about the application of what has been said. Let me repeat that the preacher does not have to deal in the pulpit with this critical differentiation of the dimensions of the picture given in Scripture of the events of salvation history. That is done in exegesis and theology, and he should know about it. His task is rather to proclaim these events in such a way that the call buried in the depth of this salvation history can reach the listener and that, in spite of all that is "wondrous" and definitely a matter of the past in this history, the listener does not experience it as something "miraculous". Perhaps the preacher could use this as a simple criterion: how would he tell the story if, expecting the consent of a reasonable faith and not relying on the inevitability and compulsion of a rationalistic and empirical attitude, he presented the event as if it had happened here and now, and not in the past?

IV

THE SPECIFIC IDIOM OF THE LANGUAGE OF PROCLAMATION

1. *Christian Proclamation as Preaching to the "Heathen"*

The preacher must "translate" into the speech of the public actually in front of him. This real "public" for our sermons is often very different from what we think it is. It would be a capital and frightening mistake and a sign of neglect in the preaching Church if we thought that the proclamation must above all be adjusted to the mentality of the so-called "good" and "believing" people who still exist here and there in constantly diminishing remnants. We must preach first of all to the "heathens" among us, and to speak their language has nothing to do with affectation and self-conscious modernity; this would only annoy the listener. When we use their language, our sermon will also help the "good" Christians because these are also men of today whose true characteristics are overlaid with traditionalisms and customary speech which prevent their mind and heart from being stirred by anything more precise in their customary way of speaking. Here it must be pointed out that a preacher cannot defend the "simplicity" of his language by referring to the "simple" people, when in fact he uses the traditional theological clichés out of laziness and for his own convenience. Even when the "ordinary people" cannot *speak* theology, they can *listen* to it and instinctively know whether the preacher in his "translation" has found a way of saying something to them

and so becomes "credible", or whether he makes it easy for himself by using jargon, whether modern or antiquated.[2]

2. Secular and Sacred Language

This translation must take place in a *religious* language. When
the preacher must speak from within the language of modern
man, this obviously does not mean that this translation may
"secularize" the content (and today there is a great danger of
this) or—and this is the essential point here—that the language
can simply remain, or even should be, "secular". This is already
ruled out by the contrast between language and meaning, and
this meaning concerns God and his relationship with man. Both
for the present and the future there must therefore be a "sacred
language". Where we are dealing not merely with scientific and
technological symbols but with the expression of man's existence, which is an enduring factor and cannot be covered by
science alone, the most simple as well as the most modern
words entail a kind of "transcendental" directness, a reference
to the mystery that we call God.

According to the circumstances we need to use taste and in-
stinct; occasionally comparisons and images from the technological world can penetrate into sacred language, and even become technically theological expressions. On the other hand,
older expressions can remain alive today, although they cannot
be wholly left without some "translation". Therefore, not every
"archaic" tendency in religious speech need necessarily be
wrong. Nor should we overlook the fact that something like the
"archetypes" of Jung may persist in modern man and may be
brought to life in sacred language. Nor does a change in language mean a complete lack of continuity and correspondence
in the languages of various ages. Otherwise the history of language would become totally incoherent, and any "understand-

[2] These principles have been dealt with in greater detail by K. Lehmann, "Some Ideas from Pastoral Theology on the Proclamation of the
Christian Message to Present-Day Unbelievers," in *Concilium* 23 (1967),
pp. 83–102.

ing" of earlier languages would become impossible. "The Lord is my Shepherd" is still intelligible today, although in our society of officialdom the word "Lord" has become obscure and most people have never seen a shepherd, so that this beautiful word has become rather pale. On the other hand, the expressed thought that people suffer from the repression of God can be full of meaning, although in this particular sense the word "repression" only dates from Freud.

Osmund Schreuder, O.F.M./*Nijmegen, Netherlands*

The Mechanics
of Preaching

There is much talk today about the "ineffectual preaching in the Churches", and the expression is hardly exaggerated. There is first of all the fact that the mass of believers have but a poor knowledge of their faith. Thus an American inquiry, based on a questionnaire about the Bible and dogma, led to the conclusion that preaching and religious instruction have very little effect. This is particularly true of Catholics.[1] Second, there is the fact that many churchgoers are manifestly dissatisfied with the sermons. Soundings taken in Holland suggest the following hypothesis: the majority accept the sermon as an institution, but they are practically incapable of repeating what they have just heard in a sermon, and they are rarely moved by it.[2] No wonder that a large number of persons who react to a written investigation—therefore a better educated and more interested group—complain bitterly about what is presented to them from the pulpit.[3] Third, the clergy themselves are by no means united in their enthusiasm. They feel,

[1] W. Schroeder and V. Obenhaus, *Religion in American Culture* (Glencoe, Ill., 1964), pp 93f.

[2] C. Straver, *Massacommunicatie en godsdienstige beinvloeding* (Hilversum, 1967), pp. 162f.

[3] This may be concluded from the not strictly scientific report on 1,200 replies to a written inquiry of the German weekly *Mann in der Zeit*, by G. Türk and J. Walter (Univ. of Würzburg).

even more strongly than the laity, that the sermon is not adequately prepared, that preaching is poor and that seminary training is very defective on this point.[4] Usually the members of a higher profession judge the quality of professional services more accurately than the clients! Hence a certain importance should be attached to the negative judgment of preachers who, for once, put the theory aside and try to get down to the facts of what the pulpit actually offers, even if they do not do so in a strictly scientific fashion.[5]

What I am going to say seems to be confirmed by more important investigations that have been conducted in France and Italy, although I have not actually seen the final conclusions.[6]

In such a situation it is understandable that, at our wit's end, we should turn to the empirical sciences. But, unfortunately, even here not much is as yet available, since socio-religious investigations began only to develop somewhat after World War II and the subject of preaching had hardly been broached. Therefore, all I can do in what follows is to make some sensible, however hypothetical, observations on this burning issue, based on research in mass communication, mainly American.

Basic Laws of Mass Communication

The means of mass communication are far from omnipotent, and the individual is not in any way defenseless. From the "sender" to the "receiver" there runs a whole chain of so-called intervening factors which have a powerful influence on the effectiveness of these media, and this to a degree which makes it impossible to look on the mass media as the necessary and sufficient explanation of what is going on in the "receiver"; the influence of these media is usually secondary. Moreover, what-

---

[4] This is the conclusion from an unpublished Dutch investigation. Cf. also J. Fichter, *Priest and People* (New York, 1965), pp. 186, 194.

[5] W. von Bissing, "Die evangelische Predigt in der modernen Gesellschaft," in *Zeitschr. f. Evang. Ethik* 51 (1961), pp. 105f.

[6] S. Burgalassi, "Aspetti psicosociologici della predicazione," in *Rivista di Sociologia* 7 (May-Aug., 1965), pp. 51–112; H. Jourde and D. Pézeril, "Dialogues sur la prédication," in *Sem. relig. de Paris* (Dec. 18, 1965), pp. 1257–80.

ever influence the media may have, it consists usually in that they confirm and reinforce what the "receiver" already thought long before. If the message transmitted does not agree with what the receiver already thought, it is either rejected or twisted in a way which confirms his view. Mass media communication can only be a primary cause and bring about change when the intervening factors themselves already point to the need for change or when the message is aimed at topics that are not related to the intervening factors and therefore belong to what is called an "ideological vacuum". This is briefly the conclusion reached by J. Klapper and drawn from 270 studies which represented a wider field of 1,000 inquiries.[7]

Mechanisms of Selection

The first group of intervening factors which strike one immediately and operate in the direction indicated above is made up of a number of selection mechanisms. The listener responds more willingly to a communication of things that agree with his views, feelings, needs and interests than those that do not. Catholics prefer to read papers and weeklies which support the same conclusions that they have. Churchgoers who are partners in a mixed marriage or who want to limit the number of their children will "switch off" more easily than others when, for instance, on the feast of the Holy Family, the sermon deals with marriage from an opposite point of view.

More important are the hardly distinguishable mechanisms of selective perception and interpretation. From one and the same communication one person picks up this point, another that, and even if the communication comes across as a whole, it is still interpreted in different ways, according to individual conviction, etc. Thus cartoons which ridicule racial or confessional prejudices are interpreted correctly by some, while others find in them a glorification of pure Americanism or Jewish inventions aimed at exploiting the tensions between various religious

[7] J. Klapper, *The Effects of Mass Communication* (Glencoe, Ill., 1960), pp. 7f.

groups. In the same way, one and the same sermon preaching genuinely evangelical conversion is understood by one, while another sees in it an unjustified criticism of the Church, and a third looks on it as an exhibition of negative moralism addressed to the "wicked world".

Lastly, I must mention the mechanism of selective memory: what one agrees with is more easily remembered than what one does not agree with, or other material.

Forms of Belief

The selection mechanisms are regulated by deeper and wider complexes. Of the greatest importance here is the function religion fulfills in the listener, and his corresponding attitude, conscious or unconscious, toward the ecclesiastical institution.[8]

For many the Church is still the institution of the *ancien régime*, the "people's Church" to which everyone must belong because she offers the individual the means of salvation and by her traditions bestows a moral order on society. In this case the ritual occupies the first place, followed by the sermon which in a certain sense has become part of the ritual. It is the Church's main task to impress upon the audience the morally valid rules of the game and to demand that these rules be obeyed for the sake of peace and order. Here the preacher has to respect the standards of the local group; he must justify the *status quo*. No one expects any kind of prophetism. One listens to things that are well known and therefore do not require much attention. However, the sermon is part of the ritual, and so the men are fully justified in taking a few minutes off and slipping out for some other way of passing the time—for instance, in the local café.

Where Catholics are a minority, the Church is no longer the institution of a local group, but rather the central organization around which a whole section of the population is gathered. Measures are taken to defend her against attacks from outside and to maintain the group intact; one fights for the Church's

[8] Cf. O. Schreuder, *Gestaltwandel der Kirche* (Olten, 1967), pp. 61f.

rights and for those of the group. It becomes a feast of orthodoxy and conformity. The sermon is important and totally inspired by the institution. It becomes a mechanism for indoctrination of both dogma and morality. The institutionalized content and norms must be known and maintained in every detail. The faithful should know what makes them different from everyone else, what is Catholic and what not. The plain and unchangeable principles of the Church must be dealt with from every concrete aspect. Problems of life, time and society are mainly tackled insofar as they are a danger to the institution and its standards. Much emphasis is placed on the formal virtues: obedience, loyalty, unity, uniformity, militancy, etc.

The "people's Church" and the minority Church are for a large part things of the past. The Catholic group is often completely integrated into society at large, the spiritual climate has become pluralistic, and tolerance has become a matter of principle. The notion of "Church" accordingly undergoes a change in the minds and hearts of the faithful. The Church becomes one of the Christian denominations which is indeed based on the Gospel but should not be absolutized. At the same time there is a great differentiation in the ties that hold the Church together.

For some the Church becomes principally an institution of service to cope with the individual spiritual and psychological needs created by the practical circumstances of life. If one thinks that the sermon has an important function, then one demands of the sermon that it be centered on the "client", be concerned with those worldly needs that beset the individual, and give help and advice in practical difficulties, consolation in disappointments, relief from the confusion of daily life and some comfort for the heart. At the same time the preacher is asked to justify the needs and interests of the faithful. There is less interest in the Bible, dogma, and moral and institutional norms. Nor do these people want to be disturbed by a theology of conversion or prophecy. If, however, the Church is seen as responsible for an evangelical ethic of brotherliness, the individual functions receive less emphasis. The sermon should then start from society. The preacher is expected to deal with these problems in the light of the Gospel; he must stimulate Christian action and a Christian transformation of the world. Here, too, there is less interest in dogma, individual morality and institutional norms. There is a great need for a justification of the social *status quo,* although protest is by no means excluded in certain cases.

A third group looks on the Church primarily as a specialized institution concerned with philosophical problems. This kind of audience demands of the sermon that it be an explanation of existence. The principal interest goes to such vast issues as the existence of God, the person of Christ, eternal life, death, and so on. The preachers must deal professionally and effectively with whatever is for sale in the philosophical market. Individual and social problems must also be treated in the light of such a theological, or biblical, "explanation of existence" (*Existenzerhellung*).

The forms of faith, as I have summarized and rather oversimplified them here, are in the nature of a hypothesis; they are not empirically verified, although some confirmation could be adduced.[9] However, if the data still to be assembled would point in the same direction, then it becomes obvious that the selection mechanisms will be operating differently according to what form of faith a particular group is inclined.

The Image of the Source of Communication

When we ask a number of persons to take part in an experiment and to arrange a series of priestly tasks in order of importance, they will do this in various ways. It then appears that there are various images of the ideal priesthood: the minister of the liturgy and the sacraments, the preacher, the counselor, the contact man in the parish, etc. And, of course, the higher one places the function of proclamation, the greater the expectations

[9] Cf. R. Köster, *Die Kirchentreuen* (Stuttgart, 1959), pp. 68f.; "L'Eglise catholique et les prêtres," in *Sondages* 24 (1962), pp. 23f.

of the sermon, the higher the demands, and the less tolerance when these expectations are frustrated.

A second relevant element lies in the scope attributed to the various tasks. In olden days the village pastor was the upholder of the social-ethical tradition of the local group and so was entitled to intervene in all kinds of affairs that concerned the village. In a minority situation the "business" of the priest had practically no limits; he seemed to be an expert in everything and was asked for advice in the most insignificant affairs.[10] Today a new distribution of competency between priest and layman has developed in many places; the priest should limit himself to what is strictly religious and ecclesiastical, the rest belongs to the autonomous layman. The priest is allowed to speak about the needs and problems of this world in the light of the Gospel, but he has no right to slip into detailed instructions or to indulge in authoritarianism.

A third influential factor is the question of the basis of authority. Those who are still living in the mentality of the "people's" or the minority Church look on the priest as being endowed, by the fact of his ordination, with a special mysterious quality which distinguishes him from everyone else and places him above everyone else (traditional authority). In performing his function he is also supported by law (legal authority). On the basis of these two assumptions his authority is accepted. But these two assumptions have lost much of their importance today. Many demand that the priest should prove his authority either by a factual qualification obtained through education (functional or professional authority) or by personal qualities which are not a mere matter of professional training and yet outstanding (charismatic authority). The nature of the authority with which the priest is credited is probably connected with the nature of the form of faith that prevails in the individual faithful. In any case, it should be clear that people will demand different things of the sermon and will interpret the sermon differently according to their particular view of the priest's authority.

[10] Cf. C. Ward, *Priests and People* (Liverpool, 1961), pp. 54f.

Apart from the ideal image, there is the empirical image of the priest. If people are convinced that, on the whole, the priests do their job properly, the climate for the sermon will be more favorable than when this is not the case. Here the experience of current preaching plays an important part. If this experience has created continuous negative attitudes in the people, even the good preacher is *a priori* faced with barriers that are difficult to overcome, barriers of purely neutral expectations or even positive resistance which will kill his attempt. The degree to which the preacher is personally known and sympathized with as a human being is also of great importance.[11] If one has come to know him in other circumstances or if one is convinced of his good intentions through a more direct personal contact, he will be more easily accepted in the pulpit, even if his sermon is not exactly ideal.

Communication in Two Stages

It is often said that the urban parish has become a number of individuals with few or no communal features. In this case there would be an almost immediate contact between the preacher and his congregation. This, however, is not probable. One of the great rediscoveries of research in mass communication is the existence of primary groups, even in the large cities. It is precisely these groups that insert themselves between the "sender" and the "receiver". They decide how effective the communication will be, and this applies to the sermon. Here the opinion leaders of the group play a crucial part. They are usually more open-minded toward the communication and are also usually better informed; they are the ones who will decide whether a communication aimed at changes will be effective or not.[12] If the preacher is determined to achieve something, he

---

[11] Cf. C. Straver, *op. cit.,* pp. 166f.

[12] Cf. J. Klapper, *op. cit.,* pp. 26f., 65f.; E. Katz and P. Lazarsfeld, *Personal Influence: The Part Played by People in the Flow of Mass Communications* (Glencoe, Ill., 1955); E. Katz, "The Two-Step Flow of Communication: An Up-To-Date Report on an Hypothesis," in *Publ. Opinion Quart.* 21 (1957), pp. 61f.

will have to take this process of the "two-step flow of communication" into account. It is not the preacher who is the key figure but the leaders of religious opinion in the small groups. He should therefore always ask himself what relevant primary groups exist in his congregation, who are the religious leaders, what the hierarchical relations are between these groups, and what his own relations are with these groups and their leaders: is he well known by them or not, are there close links or is there a certain distance, has he any prestige or not, can he rely on sympathy or must he face antipathy, etc.?

Cognitive Dissonances

The Christian lives in a pluralistic society, and in the forum of philosophy and attitudes toward life he gets acquainted with contradictory opinions about God, Christ, death, the Church, etc. He is also faced with the tension which exists between the Christian ideals that he believes in and the poor, difficult, perhaps impossible realization of these ideals in his own life and his social environment. His consciousness therefore contains conflicting contents in which he is personally involved; this is what is meant by "cognitive dissonances". These create a psychical discomfort which he wants to shake off. Sometimes he will start looking for solutions by gathering information. This gives the preacher a chance because there is an explicit demand for "answers". It is therefore often worthwhile to link up with these "dissonances" and even to mention them explicitly at the beginning of the sermon so that he can create an "ideological vacuum" which must be filled. This is the way clever advertisers and political propaganda always work.

This "conflict method", however, will only be effective when it is used expertly. There is no point in treating of problems that may interest the theologians but not the ordinary faithful. It is also a mistake for a preacher to explain his own problems of faith from the pulpit without asking himself whether the congregation has the same problems. It is equally pointless—e.g., in a dialogue sermon—to let one of the preachers act as the "advocate of the devil" and make such an overwhelming case for the problem that the other cannot possibly solve it. Moreover, it is important not to give an answer to the problem which presents the faithful with an impossible task, because this would only increase the discomfort experienced in the dissonances and frighten them away from any further information—i.e., any other sermon.[18]

Conclusions

We will bring these various considerations to a close with a few general conclusions affecting pastoral work.

1. The effectiveness of preaching depends for the greatest part on the intervening factors. We should therefore not overrate the possibilities contained in the traditional ways of preaching. Hence, all pastoral work that limits itself—as is so often the case—to the Word and the liturgy within the church building is seriously defective. In other words, to identify the notion of proclamation with the traditional forms in which this proclamation took place is simply to misunderstand the reality of the situation.

2. Pastoral work with the small group, or "group proclamation", is one of the most important tasks of the parish priest and the laity who assist him. Hence we need discussion groups, discussion evenings and group work. By these "group methods" I do not mean organizing the parish in artificial groups, regardless of natural ties (separation of men and women, meeting in the parochial hall, etc.), nor entertaining the group with lectures followed by questions to be answered by the leader. It would be better to follow the modern American group methods, of which we have very little experience in Europe. To learn about them should be part of the training of every pastor and every layman who wishes to take a leading part in the work of the parish. There is room here to develop this.[14]

---

[18] For a detailed analysis of the theory, see L. Festinger, *The Theory of Cognitive Dissonance* (Stanford, California, [2]1962).

[14] The relation of faithful to the Church is becoming more and more one of dialogue; cf. H. Schelsky, "Ist die Dauerreflexion institutional-

3. The priest should work diligently to improve his "image", particularly the empirical image of the priest. In order to be able to preach effectively, he must again become a socially recognizable figure, even in the large city. If people have come to know and appreciate him at a personal level, he will find that his sermons carry greater weight. This implies constant and systematic contact with every natural group in the parish. We should beware of deceiving ourselves by pointing to the vast scope of the urban parish and the shortage of priests. I know from personal experience that it is possible in an urban parish with one priest per four thousand Catholics, of whom one-third are practicing Catholics, to visit within one year at least two-thirds of the practicing households in a way which allows discussion of religion and the Church, so that such a visit can fulfill the function of individual preaching. Rather, the difficulties here are lack of understanding the importance of this task, bad visiting techniques (which most priests, unfortunately, have never overcome), and the disinclination to leave other, often pleasanter and more lucrative tasks to others, particularly the laity. If a priest does not wish to begin with this, perhaps under the guise of "theological" arguments, he will create a social distance between himself and the faithful which will undermine all his pastoral work in the Church disastrously.

4. The preacher must explain the religious meaning of everyday life, and many today stress that he must recognize the value of the world in its own right, that he must start from the world, that he must preach a Christianity that is relevant within this world. This may conceal a grave danger. By exaggerating the principle, the preacher, whose words are already understood as mainly an attempt at justification, will degrade the proclamation to the level of an ideology of the needs and interests of his audience, a systematic justification of the *status quo* in a middle-class society, a merely cultural religion. Like the managers of

---

isierbar?" in *Zeitschr. f. Evang. Ethik* 1 (1957), pp. 153f.; Eng. tr.: "Can Continual Reflection Be Institutionalized?" in *Cross Currents* 15 (1965), pp. 171f.

institutes of mass communication, the preacher runs the risk of
adjusting his "product" too uncritically to the needs and interests of this particular religious "market".[15] On the other hand,
there is little point in sounding a "prophetic" protest when one
is soaked in the mentality of a "people's" or minority Church.
The social changes simply force the churchgoing people to accept other forms of faith.[16] The days of ritualism, moralism,
dogmatism and institutionalism are over. It is just as pointless
to withdraw into a shell of "pure religion". Nor will the audience
swallow exaggerated professional theology or exegesis. It would
seem to me that one could avoid both extremes of "pure justification" and "pure prophecy" by linking the sermon to the tensions experienced in the ordinary Christian life of every day.
Within this framework a theory of "cognitive dissonances",
worked out with reference to preaching, could be of great
service.

Finally, the too comprehensive character of this article is
partly the result of the fact that we know very little about the
reality of the Church's preaching. A realistic approach can only
be built up when we have far more data at our disposal. Therefore, priests at every level of the hierarchy should be willing to
cooperate with such research, without being afraid of "giving
themselves away". Whoever wants to improve the quality of his
pastoral service should become aware of the effectiveness of his
actual performance with the help of such expert research.

[15] This opinion is empirically supported in a study of written preaching by L. Schneider and S. Dornbusch, *Popular Religion* (Chicago,
1958).

[16] O. Schreuder, *op. cit.*, pp. 41f.

Yves Congar, O.P./*Strasbourg, France*

Sacramental Worship and Preaching

The days are gone when one could oppose a (Protestant) Church of the Word to a (Catholic) Church of the sacrament, and attribute the efficacy of grace to the Word according to Scripture, or to the sacrament according to the Church. In various countries the liturgical movement was supported by a biblical movement and often accompanied by a search for a renewed preaching and catechetics. In this way it brought the celebration of the sacraments and the preaching of the Word together into a coherent whole.

I

WORD AND SACRAMENT IN THE THEOLOGY OF VATICAN COUNCIL II

Vatican Council II set its seal on this movement, not only in its *Constitution on the Sacred Liturgy,* but also by its teaching on the priesthood of bishops and priests and on the catechumenate in missionary work. Four points are particularly noteworthy in this work of the Council:

1. *The sovereign position of Christ as the prime author of all communication of salvation.* With this goes the recognition of various modes of Christ's presence,[1] modes which must not be

[1] Cf. *Constitution on the Sacred Liturgy,* n. 7.

51

isolated from one another, although they must be distinguished because they are the modes of presence and action of the same one Lord and all aim at the same end, the full realization of the new and definitive covenant.

2. *The reintegration of the Word into the celebration of the liturgy*[2] *and in the definition of the priestly ministry, whether of the bishop or the simple priest.* We shall see later how this affects the definition of the ministerial priesthood itself. But we should note at once that this goes much further than a mere increase in the *part* played by the Word in the celebration. It is not a question of quantity but of the constitutive elements, the very nature, of the celebration—in any case, of the full celebration.

3. *The integration of a scriptural value into the very notion of the liturgy or of Christian worship at large.* Dom Odo Casel had already brought this point to light and it was accepted fully in the encyclical *Mediator Dei*—namely, that the Christian liturgy or cult is an acceptance of a gift bestowed on us by God in and through Jesus Christ before it can be a movement from us toward God (adoration, offering, praise, thanksgiving). Now, if it is true that the Word did not only become Word but flesh, and the sacramental signs are rooted in this *incarnation,* it is also true that (a) the biblical meaning of "Word", *dabar,* embraces both the aspect of an effective action and that of presenting it to our knowledge, and (b) the Word of God, as operative in the Church, is *also* an *opus Dei,* a work of God, to the extent precisely that it is the Word *of God,* a point elaborated particularly by J. Betz and O. Semmelroth (cf. bibliography). Most Catholic theologians today attribute a certain sacramental structure to the Word of God in the sense of being an observable sign through which the God of grace works our salvation. It is true that this happening of grace is less assured and more linked with the person of the minister than in the sacraments strictly so called where Christ alone operates.

[2] *Ibid.,* esp. nn. 6, 35, 52, 56.

4. The Council has renewed our view of the Church mainly by stressing that the Church is the People of God and a kind of universal sacrament of salvation. Without adopting a particular school of thought, it has established the idea of the general sacramentality of the Church. One may agree with the Protestant theologian, J. J. von Allmen, when he says that if the Church is not aware of the fact of having a mission toward the world in the midst of which she lives, "the sacrament tends to withdraw into the sacraments in the plural".[3] But when the Church is conscious of living in a wholly missionary situation, the perspective of a salvation history in progress will turn its attention to Christ as the sacrament of God (the "mystery", as St. Paul speaks of it) and to the Church as the sacrament of Christ. This should not, of course, make us lose a clear awareness of the specific character of the classic seven sacraments, but one should not isolate this concept or extol it to such a degree that we overlook the whole sacramental reality consisting of Christ and all that he does in and through the Church in view of our sanctification and God's glory. In this respect, the Word stands side by side with the sacraments. The rich word "mystery", which is more comprehensive than "sacrament" as understood in the West, embraces both the aspect of knowledge and that of action, the professed or proclaimed faith and the celebration of the great events that are the principles of our salvation.

II

ANALYSIS OF THE CHRISTIAN CONCEPT OF WORSHIP

These various considerations exclude any separation of cult or sacrament from the proclamation of God's Word; they rather confirm the need for integration. For an explanation and justification in depth of this need, we must analyze the notion of worship or cult itself, not in general or of any kind of worship,

---

[3] *Prophétisme sacramental* (Neuchâtel-Paris, 1964), p. 12.

but of Christian worship as such. This Christian cult has three characteristic features.

1. *Christian Worship as a Living Anamnesis (Commemoration)*

Christian worship took over, in new conditions, the character of Jewish worship as an *anamnesis* (i.e., an actualizing memory, or active representation) of the acts by which God intervened in order to make a covenant with us and to save us. In contrast with the various kinds of nature worship of the surrounding peoples and even of those whose country was occupied by Israel, and in spite of the fact that the Israelites mixed with those people without losing their identity, though sometimes tempted to adopt their rites, Jewish worship was a celebration of the great facts, the *magnalia Dei,* by which Yahweh constituted himself their God and made them his people: the deliverance from servitude and the Pasch, the giving of the law (Pentecost) and the conclusion of the covenant, etc. The psalms constantly celebrate all this and they are still the basis of our clerical prayer. Now exegesis has shown that all this is much more than a mere "reminding"; it is rather an actualization of divine acts which, having happened once, keep their operative value for the believers of all ages, who make them actual again in the Spirit when they celebrate these acts in faith and thanksgiving.

Christians recognize the typological value of these great acts of God in the old covenant, but they go beyond this and celebrate the event of Jesus Christ, with all that this implies for us, in his incarnation, his baptism, his passion and resurrection, followed by Pentecost—all events that are celebrated each year in the liturgical seasons and each day in the eucharist (see the *Unde et memores* of the Canon). The unique facts of the history of salvation are constantly actualized in the natural cycle of the seasons. *All* the sacraments refer to the "Pasch" of the Lord, his passion and resurrection, and apply this to the decisive moments of man's life. That is why the eucharist is their common central point, since it is the celebration of the Pasch of Jesus and of the new covenant, concluded in his blood.

Thus the liturgy is by itself both proclamation and preaching.[4] This value of the celebration as an announcement, a Word, has been powerfully strengthened since the anaphora is now pronounced in a language accessible to all; the Mass has again become in the full sense an "announcing of the death of the Lord until he comes" (1 Cor. 11, 26). Thus Vatican Council II filled the gap which existed between a didactic part, in the vernacular, and a sacramental part for which we used a language that was called "sacred".[5] The liturgy preaches in words and in actions, with an authoritativeness and power which no sermon can ever equal. That is why it remains the great living instruction of the Church, as Pius XI said, the great means to educate and nourish our faith.

Nevertheless, the incomparable insights contained in the liturgy, which are to be transmitted, are more or less veiled; the way in which sacraments like the anointing of the sick, holy orders, penance or marriage refer to the Pasch of Christ is not immediately clear. Moreover, the liturgical forms and texts were immobilized; they have been the same since the Fathers, for all people and whatever their condition, in festivity or in trouble, in power or suffering oppression, whether they are children or adults, uncouth or refined. It therefore inevitably needs adaptation and suitable application. It must be extended and completed by a mode of expression that suits the place, the

[4] Cf. *Constitution on the Sacred Liturgy*, n. 33: "For in the liturgy God speaks to his people and Christ is still proclaiming his Gospel." Also cf. n. 35.

[5] Here we might recall St. Methodius' introduction of the Slavonic language in Moravia. Although Pope Hadrian II had approved his initiative, Methodius was called to Rome by John VIII in 879. He was allowed to preach and celebrate the first part of the Mass in "barbaric" language, on the basis of Ps. 116, 1 and Phil. 2, 11, but he was told to celebrate the sacramental part in Latin or Greek (cf. Jaffé, *Mon. Germ. Hist., Epist. VII*, p. 161). The saint was soon allowed to celebrate the whole liturgy in Slavonic (Letter of June, 880 to the Count of Moravia (Jaffé, *op. cit.*, p. 223, where the same texts are quoted with the addition of Acts 2, 11 and 1 Corinthians 14, 4. This was strengthened by the argument that God had created all languages in praise of his glory; this was confirmed by a letter from John VIII to Methodius, March 23, 881 (Jaffé, *op. cit.*, pp. 243–44).

time and the people. This is the function of the homily which, according to the *Constitution on the Sacred Liturgy* (nn. 35, 52), must accompany every public celebration except for a serious reason. It is also most desirable that the celebration of the other sacraments not only be as intelligible as possible but also that it be preceded or accompanied by some words of explanation or adaptation. The present reform of the liturgy aims at making the acts of worship not merely some reality in their own right but acts of living people who feel involved in them. This supposes that between the fixed form of the liturgy on the one hand, and the spirit and freedom of specific people in a given situation on the other, there must be the mediation of a Word. When this Word has its official place in the celebration, it becomes an integral part of the liturgical action (*Constitution on the Sacred Liturgy,* nn. 35, 52, 56).

2. *The Sacraments of Faith*

All worship is the expression of a conviction about a transcendent and invisible being, and as such can be defined as a *protestatio fidei,* a witness to faith. In pagan worship, however, this word "faith" would only have a weak, analogical or purely psychological sense, as there it would not be a matter of faith in a living and active God who takes initiatives that concern me and who wants to establish a personal relationship with me; it would be a *religion* by which man tries to predispose a personified force of nature in his favor. In the (Jewish-) Christian religion the place or means of man's encounter with God is the historical reality of the initiatives taken by the living God. Here religion lies within a *faith* through which I yield to those initiatives and apply them to myself. Faith is my response to God's action communicated to me through his Word. Christian worship is therefore a *protestatio fidei,* a *witness* to faith, in the strongest sense of that word. That is the way St. Thomas Aquinas speaks of it.

St. Thomas also favors an expression, already traditional in his time—namely, that of calling the sacraments "sacraments of faith".[6] The liturgical Constitution explains this expression as follows: "They [the sacraments] not only presuppose faith, but by words and objects they also nourish, strengthen and express it" (n. 59). This means that faith and sacraments or liturgy are wholly intermingled in a process where faith precedes, accompanies and expresses itself in the celebration, and comes out of it expanded, nourished and fortified.

Theology tells us that the sacraments derive all their efficacy from the Pasch of Christ, but they can only do so when *linked* with this Pasch, not only by the fact that the Lord himself instituted them but by faith. Only faith, indeed, establishes that saving *contact*. This comes out so expressively in the Gospel passage about the woman who suffered from a hemorrhage (Mt. 9, 20–21; Mk. 5, 25–34; Lk. 8, 43–48). Jesus was surrounded and even pressed by a whole crowd, and yet only the woman who approached him with faith really *touched* him. St. Augustine explains this passage in this sense[7] and St. Thomas constantly attributes to faith this power to establish the necessary contact which allows Christ's passion to be effectively applied to us.[8] That is why he can say that "all the sacraments derive their efficacy from the faith".[9] The faith he refers to is essentially the faith of the Church as such.[10] The minister is the channel of that faith, and we know that the validity of the sacrament only requires that he has the intention "to do what the Church does".

It is obvious that, from the point of view of the building up of the body of Christ in the individual and in the community,

[6] Cf. J. Gaillard, "Les sacrements de la foi," in *Rev. Thom.* 59 (1959), pp. 5–31, 270–309; L. Villette (see bibliography), II, p. 17, n. 1

[7] Tract. XXVI, *In Evang. Ioann.* 3 (*PL* 35, c. 1608).

[8] Cf., *e.g., IV Sent.*, d. 4, q. 3, art. 2, sol. 2.

[9] *IV Sent.*, d. 1, q. 2, art. 6, ad 3; J. Gaillard, *art. cit.*, p. 276; L. Villette, *op. cit.*, I, pp. 233f.

[10] Cf. J. Gaillard, "S. Augustin et les sacrements de la foi. Verbum fidei in Ecclesia Dei," in *Rev. Thom.* 59 (1959), pp. 664–703; L. Villette, *op. cit.* I, pp. 243–54; II, pp. 56–67, 71, 75–79, 371. In the case of infant baptism this faith of the Church works by itself, with the institution and the effective promise of the Lord, without the personal faith of the baptized person playing a part.

the minister's faith, as expressed in his whole behavior, his way of celebrating and his words, is most important. The priest is not only a representative of the "Church", but he exercises a kind of spiritual paternity by faith and Word. He does not only have faith for himself; the others lean on his faith and profit by it. The faith of the faithful also enters into the sacramental process, not as *constituting* the sacrament, as is the case for the faith of the Church (except in the sacrament of penance), but as a disposition for the reception of the sacrament and as making it possible to profit by it spiritually. In this way the faith of the faithful is involved in the sacrament they receive; it is necessary *before,* in order to have the right disposition, stimulate the desire to receive it and open the soul to Christ's action; *during* the reception, in order to take a full part in it by giving the sacramental rite its spiritual meaning; and *after* the reception in order to receive the fruit of the sacrament fully and—in the eucharist, for example—to ensure that the *sacramental consumption,* which is carnal, signifies and effects the *spiritual consumption.*[11] For this very reason the real or effective reception of the sacrament provides the faithful with a support that may be compared to that of a presence in our emotional life. One profits from the sacrament through faith, but faith, in turn, is nourished by the sacrament. It is a continuous process where the two elements support one another.

It is obvious that if faith is thus involved in the celebration, it is most important that a homily accompany this celebration and that, where this is the case, this homily be part of the celebration. The homily contributes to the establishment of the truth of the celebration. By itself the liturgy consists already of both words and gestures. Therefore it ensures by itself this rousing of the faith which its purpose requires. It is in danger, however, of being too impersonal, too little "actual", to ensure

[11] Cf. St. Thomas, *Sum. theol.* III, q. 80, art. 1; *In Ev. Ioann.,* c. 6, lect. 7, n. 2. Hence the famous "Crede et manducasti" ("Believe and you have eaten") of St. Augustine, *In Ev. Ioann.,* tr. XXV, 12 and XXVI, 11–12 (*PL* 35, cc. 1602, 1611–12).

this to the full. One may think, for instance, of the part played by the words of the priest in the exercise of the ministry of penance; the words personalize what the rite expresses in a common and general way.

3. The Spiritual Offering of the Christian's Life in Practice

Christian worship is a spiritual worship. It undoubtedly presumes the use of outward things; it involves our body and all our senses. It is not spiritual because it is bodiless, but because of its main content. It does not consist in *things,* but in the union of man's heart with God through faith and love. The Gospel takes over the lesson of the prophets who demanded the primacy of the sacrifice of ourselves in filial obedience, full of the love of God. The New Testament speaks about our self-sacrifice, of offering our whole bodily existence as a spiritual sacrifice acceptable to God through Jesus Christ (Rom. 12, 1; 1 Pet. 2, 5; cf. Heb. 9, 14). To this is added the sacrifice of praise (Heb. 13, 15) and that of pleasing God (Phil. 4, 18; Heb. 13, 16). The apostle himself celebrates the liturgy by bringing men to the obedience of faith (Rom. 1, 9; 15, 16; Phil. 2, 17). Vatican Council II has incorporated this apostolic teaching in what it says about the spiritual priesthood of the faithful (which is nowhere called metaphorical). It is their whole life, even "their ordinary married and family life, their daily occupations, their mental and physical relaxation", which constitutes the matter of the Christian's spiritual sacrifice, if all this is done in the Spirit (*Constitution on the Church,* n. 34).

But if Christian worship consists in the personal relationship between God and man himself—not in things nor even in the ceremonies as such—this can only be in a manner wholly dependent on Christ and that perfect filial relationship with God as he lived it, and this supremely in the suffering of his blessed passion and death. Now this filial relationship, this offering and this sacrifice have been given us so that we should unite ourselves with them, not only at the level of remembrance and exemplar, but in their concrete reality, in the celebration of the eucharist. Hence Christian worship consists, at the heart of its truth, in accepting gratefully this gift of God and in uniting to it that spiritual offering of our concrete and total existence. That is why priests are ordained not so much "to say Mass" as to make the faithful commune in this worship of Jesus Christ, of which they celebrate the *anamnesis* sacramentally. Such is the teaching of the Council.[12] The very logic of the sacrament demands this, but this imposes on the celebrating priest something that goes beyond the ritual celebration. Undoubtedly, there are many ways of linking the sacramental celebration with the life of people which must become their spiritual sacrifice. The entire range of activities of a parish can contribute to this—the singing, the notices, the parochial bulletin, and particularly the catechetical formation—but it is specifically the function of the homily, and the homily need not be lengthy to achieve this purpose (although it has other purposes, too, such as instruction).

Preaching as a liturgical action is indeed a commentary on the mystery that is celebrated according to the liturgical season, but it must also help the faithful to unite their life as an offering to the sacrifice of Jesus Christ. What does "life" mean here? It does not refer to an empty framework of existence, a kind of general and anonymous spiritual life, nor does it refer to what remains of man's life after everything that really interests him has been eliminated; rather, it refers to life as filled or crossed by all kinds of events, great or small, a life that is committed to the conditions and tasks of every day. The priestly homily which must accompany the celebration explains the mystery on the basis of the liturgical texts, but it must aim at bringing the faithful into this mystery by accepting, and throwing light on, their life so that they can unite it to this mystery. When this happens, the sermon is truly a Word which prompts a response.

[12] Cf. *Constitution on the Church*, n. 28; *Decree on the Ministry and Life of Priests*, nn. 2, 5.

III

Two Applications

In conclusion, I would like to apply what has been said to two far-reaching subjects.

1. The Theological Concept of the Priesthood

First of all, let us consider the notion of the priesthood itself. On several occasions Vatican Council II uses the expression "true priests of the New Testament" (*veri sacerdotes Novi Testamenti*). This reveals a discreet reaction against a long-standing habit of attaching the ministry of our priesthood to that of Aaron. Now the New Testament can be described by the fact that, in contrast with the Old Testament, the prophetic and sacrificial (sacerdotal) functions are intertwined, just as the synagogue (the place for praise and teaching) and the temple (the place for sacrifices) have become one and the same in our churches. This is so because, as St. Thomas says, the sacrifice we offer is spiritual.[13] One could just as well say that because the priesthood of the New Testament is prophetical, the cult it celebrates is a cult of faith. Therefore, just as Vatican Council II reintegrated preaching into the liturgical action, so it extended the definition of the priestly ministry by the offering of the eucharistic sacrifice and revealed the priest as committed first of all to the Word, like the apostles, in cooperation with the bishops.[14] We should renew our understanding of the evan-

---

[13] *Sum. theol.* II-II, q. 102, art. 4, ad. 3.

[14] *Decree on the Ministry and Life of Priests*, n. 2, quoting Romans 15, 16. Afterward, in n. 4, the Decree speaks of the priest as the minister of the Word of God, and says: "In the Christian community itself, on the other hand, especially for those who seem to have little understanding or belief underlying their practice, the preaching of the Word is required for the sacramental ministry itself, since the sacraments are sacraments of faith drawing their origin and nourishment from the Word. This is of paramount importance in the case of the liturgy of the Word within the celebration of the Mass where there is an inseparable union of the proclamation of the Lord's death and resurrection, the response of its hearers and the very offering itself by which Christ con-

gelical priesthood on those lines, and since, again according to the Council, the formation of priests must be a lasting one, we should remember the effort necessary to evoke faith and the training that is required if that faith is to be up-to-date as the modern world demands. I could quote a whole series of ancient texts,[15] all saying more or less that if in one country Mass was celebrated for thirty years without preaching and in another there was preaching for thirty years without the Mass, people would be more Christian in the country where there was preaching.

2. *The Importance of Signs and Gestures*

The second application is still more directly concerned with pastoral work. However important preaching may be, one cannot make Christians merely by sermons. Great educationists like St. Jean-Baptiste de la Salle took care to join the liturgical celebration to their instruction in the formation of children. The lessons contained in objects, gestures and outward signs have great educational power because man is substantially both body and spirit. Truths reach him and can fully develop in him only if they touch the body; this is also why the sacrament is more complete than the simple spiritual union in the mystery.[16] Christ himself is not only the Word sent by the Father to the world but also the body, immolated and surrendered (cf. Semmelroth, in the bibliography). It would therefore be wise to choose from our theology, and from local customs connected with it, a small number of *gestures* which translate and inculcate a few basic attitudes in Christian practice. They would lay the foundation for training men as Christians.

---

firmed the new covenant in his blood. In this offering the faithful share both by their sacrificial sentiments and by the reception of the sacrament."

[15] Humbert of Romans (13th cent.), St. Bernardinus of Sienna (15th cent.), Johann Eck (16th cent.), and others.

[16] Cf. St. Thomas, *Sum. theol.* III, qu. 62, art. 6, and our study, "Les deux formes du Pain de vie dans l'Evangile et dans la Tradition," in *Sacerdoce et laïcat* (Paris, 1962), pp. 123–60.

BRIEF BIBLIOGRAPHY

1. *On the General Theme of Word and Sacrament:*

G. Söhngen, *Symbol und Wirklichkeit im Kultmysterium* (Bonn, 1937); Congress of Strassburg, *Parole de Dieu et Liturgie* (Paris, 1958); J. Betz, "Wort und Sakrament. Versuch einer dogmatischen Verhältnisbestimmung," in *Verkündigung und Glaube* (Freiburg, 1958), pp. 76–99; L. Villette, *Foi et sacrement*, 2 vols. (Paris, 1959 and 1964); E. Schillebeeckx, *De sacramentele Heilseconomie* (Antwerp, 1952); *idem, Christ, the Sacrament of the Encounter with God* (London, 1963); *idem,* "Parole et sacrement dans l'Eglise," in *Lumière et vie* 46 (1960), pp. 25–45. O. Semmelroth, *Wirkendes Wort* (Frankfurt a. M., 1962); H. Fries (ed.), *Wort und Sakrament* (Kösel, 1966) (a collection of relevant articles taken from the *Handbuch theologischer Grundbegriffe*); H. Manders, "The Relation between Baptism and Faith," in *Concilium* 22 (1967), pp. 4–15.

2. *On the Value of "Anamnesis" in the Worship of the People of God:*

N. D. Dahl, "Anamnesis," in *Studia Theologica* 1 (1948), pp. 69–75; J. Daniélou, *Sacramentum futuri* (Paris, 1950); M. Thurian, *L'Eucharistie. Mémorial du Seigneur Sacrifice d'action de grâce et d'intercession* (Neuchâtel and Paris, 1959); H. Gross, "Zum Wurzel *szr,*" in *Biblische Zeitschr.* 4 (1960), pp. 227–37; H. Zirker, *Die kultische Vergegenwärtigung der Vergangenheit in den Psalmen* (Bonn, 1964).

3. *Some Studies on Preaching of the Liturgy:*

J. Leclercq, "Le sermon, acte liturgique," in *La Maison Dieu* 8 (1946), pp. 27–46; D. Barsotti, *Il mistero cristiano e la Parola di Dio* (Florence, 1954); H. Schlier, *Die Verkündigung im Gottesdienste der Kirche* (Cologne, 1953), reproduced in *Die Zeit der Kirche* (Freiburg, 1958); Congress of Strassburg, *Parole de Dieu et liturgie* (Paris, 1958); W. Kahles, "Glaubensverkündigung aus dem Geiste der Liturgie," in *Archiv f. Liturgiewiss.* 2 (1959–60), pp. 417–54. L. Bouyer, *Sens de la vie sacerdotale* (Tournai, 1960), pp. 34f.; *idem, Parole, Eglise, Sacrements dans le Catholicisme et le Protestantisme* (Paris, 1960); J. Wagner, "La fonction de la prédication dans la liturgie," in *Parole de Dieu et Sacerdoce* (Paris-Tournai, 1962), pp. 179–94; H. Oster, "Aujourd'hui s'accomplit le passage de l'Ecriture que vous venez d'entendre," *ibid.,* pp. 195–213.

Franz Böckle/*Bonn, W. Germany*

Moral Sermons and Urgent Moral Issues

oral sermons are in general no longer popular, but the treatment of moral issues as part of the Church's proclamation of the Word is perhaps more urgent than ever before. The development that has taken place in culture and thought has created a situation where man has to act responsibly under wholly new conditions. We must therefore start with this new situation if we want to find out which moral issues are particularly relevant for our preaching.

I

THE CHANGE IN THE SITUATION

1. A first and fundamental typical feature of the changed situation may be described as the *desacralization of nature.* This expression is not meant to cover the whole extent of what is called the secularized world but only one specific aspect of actual reality as modern man experiences it. Practically all the things we deal with in our daily existence belong to a world as man has planned and changed it, and not in the natural state in which God created it. The development of the various branches of science makes man increasingly aware of this fact. The methods used make it possible for man to grasp an in-

creasing number of elements of this reality, both macrocosmic and microcosmic. But what we can grasp with our mind, we can calculate. The result is that an increasing part of the future can be foreseen and brought closer.

All this has made it possible to extend our control and transformation of reality in a way which was never possible in the past. Our generation lives with the thought that practically anything can be achieved by man, and this thought, often running on the lines of a one-sided materialism, is easily linked with the Utopian thought that we can create a painless reality.[1] The more we penetrate into this reality, the more it loses its numinous qualities and the taboos that sprang from these qualities. While a pre-rational understanding of nature inclined man to personalize it and to use it as a foundation for his moral behavior by making it a norm for himself and his situation, science is desacralizing this nature. But this desacralization is immediately followed by a "demoralization"; in other words, what is not human in nature is no longer seen as constituting a norm for human moral behavior. This process is not wholly new in the history of culture, but it is sharply pointed in our "enlightened" age.

In this situation the believing Christian thinks back to what is unalterable in his picture of the world, and then he realizes that the biblical idea of creation witnesses precisely to the fact that the world is not God. Belief in God the creator confesses that God is the ultimate and transcendental ground of all empirical reality. It is precisely this absolute supremacy of God over the world which, in its transcendence, leaves the world free for an unlimited exploration of the laws of its existence. It is this light which the dogma of creation throws on the situation that makes nature truly lose all those numinous qualities, all that "absolutizing" and all the taboos that are embodied in it. "In this light of the biblical message the world is not that sovereign encompassing reality which locks man up in its pre-fixed order, but it is simply what man can hold in his hands, the

---

[1] Cf. D. von Oppen, *Zeitschr. Ev. Ethik* IV (1965), pp. 242f.

material with which he works out his humanization in history before God through a reverend use of it in Jesus Christ." [2]

In more concrete terms this means: (a) man's total dependence on God does not exclude man's own responsibility for the shaping of this world but implies it; (b) the existing reality, including man's own physiological nature, can only acquire moral significance through the human person. On the one hand we must maintain that an ethics of exclusively personal relationships, of the formal intersubjective relations between I and Thou, is an illusion, even in the views developed by social ontology, because human relationships always have a reference to things. On the other hand, however, it also remains true that only personal relationships can give this connection with things any true moral purpose. Man can only realize himself when he rationalizes and humanizes the whole field of creation, patiently and laboriously.

2. A second characteristic feature of our situation lies in *the growing awareness of man's and the world's historicity.* This is truly a phenomenon with many facets. It touches the ontology of the human person. The definition of human existence as that of a bodily-spiritual creature includes time, and this inevitably brings with it historicity and all that this implies. *Concilium* has frequently pointed to the importance of historicity for the renewal of moral theology, as, for example, in the articles by Walgrave,[3] Lobo,[4] Cox,[5] van Melsen,[6] Dolch,[7] and Rahner.[8] These contributions show clearly that this question of historicity is hardly exhausted when we say that every man must build his own future in his own present time with the heritage of the

[2] J. B. Metz, *Weltverständnis i. Glauben* (Mainz, 1965), p. 53.
[3] "Is Morality Static or Dynamic?" in *Concilium* 5 (1965), pp. 22–38.
[4] "Toward a Morality Based on the Meaning of History: The Condition and Renewal of Moral Theology," in *Concilium* 25 (1967), pp. 23–46.
[5] "Evolutionary Progress and Christian Promise," in *Concilium* 26 (1967), pp. 35–48.
[6] "Natural Law and Evolution," in *Concilium* 26 (1967), pp. 49–60.
[7] "Sin in an Evolutive World," in *Concilium* 26 (1967), pp. 75–84.
[8] "Evolution and Original Sin," in *Concilium* 26 (1967), pp. 61–74.

past. The aspects of social ethics and salvation history are far more important than the individual ethics of this point of view.

In the center of the great cultural controversies of our age lies the problem of the laws and factors that shape the human society, and behind this problem lies the search for a meaning of human history at large. That is why during the next decade "eschatology, or the understanding of the Christian promise, will exercise the brains of the best theologians".[9] Even a comprehensive and radical secularization of culture, as it has gone on for over a century, is unable to explain away religious ideas. Free from religious consciousness, they live on in a profane form as basic motives in the situation and as basic elements in the explanation of life. Cox has mentioned the eschatological elements in contemporary thought in his article. It is the task of Christianity to exploit the best elements in its tradition in order to expose the roaming demons of a nihilistic or romantic apocalyptic view of the world. In the same way Christian theology must come to terms in a critical way with Utopias of the future which belong purely to this world. In the Christian view the new age stretches back into the old and overcomes it. This promise makes the believer responsible for the renewal of the world in the spirit of the Sermon on the Mount and in freedom.

3. Finally, a third characteristic feature of our situation lies in the awareness that *in the history of culture the norms that dominate the social relationships can vary.* This insight is not new in itself, but special methods of modern social anthropology have examined and confirmed the fact. This gives those who are not initiated the impression of a far-reaching breakdown of all norms. That is an exaggeration. While an extreme situation ethics placed the individual in his uniqueness in the center and interpreted the courage to go against the norms of social morality as a noble expression of freedom, today cultural sociology makes it quite clear that man needs valid social norms if he wants to survive at all.

Whatever reasons the various schools of thought adduce in

⁹ Harvey Cox, *art. cit.,* p. 35.

proof of this fact, they are all agreed that it is a fact. Binding norms for human relationships play a vital part in the social life of man: they provide security, relieve him of many a burden and so are, for a large part, the condition for his freedom. But the universal function of these norms leaves room for a relatively large variety of concrete norms. In other words, the security, unburdening and liberation of man can be meaningfully achieved through very different sets of concrete norms. The number of things that can be reasonably regulated in similar fashion in all existing cultures is in fact rather small. This is no doubt influenced by the fact that the concept of man's freedom and dignity is not everywhere at such a high level as it is by our standards. But a sound development of norms within a given culture depends on a series of factors and laws; it would appear to be a very important task of Christian ethics that we become familiar with these regulating factors so that Christians can plant these basic Christian convictions about the dignity of man in a given society as if they were that society's very own maxims. It is high time for moral theology to stop being concerned only, or even mainly, with individual ethics— how far the individual Christian can go this way or that, or what he should do to achieve his own perfection. The task of Christian moral teaching lies in coming to terms, in a critical and constructive way, with the social ideas and norms of every age and culture.

II

THE MOST IMPORTANT ISSUES

The situation which I have described above shows a definite urgency in certain issues which belong to the field of fundamental ethics (the doctrine of principles). Burning practical questions should as far as possible be treated in connection with, and as illustrative of, these main themes. Insofar as basic issues are concerned, the following are urgent.

1. *The Changeability of Morality*

Even open-minded Catholics, who generally welcome a development in the Church's teaching on concrete moral issues, nevertheless find it hard to understand how the Church's judgment in moral questions can change so much that something, counted up to now as a mortal sin, can suddenly no longer be a mortal sin. Many experience this difficulty even when such purely positive regulations are changed as cremation and fasting. They find it particularly difficult to understand when definite points of behavior that previously were considered as *bad in themselves* and therefore forbidden under any circumstances are suddenly judged in a different way (e.g., methods of birth control). It should be stressed here that such Catholics are not really primarily concerned about whether such a new view is in fact right. Many faithful may have held this new view already for some time; in many cases their personal moral judgment has already become emancipated from the official view. But in their ecclesiastical sacramental practice they conform to the view that was preached before. The authoritative formation of the conscience in the instructions about confession is here often decisive for the rest of a person's life. For these people the Church is a kind of archetype that must look after the stability of order and morals. Therefore, when norms are changed which were proclaimed with a more authoritarian emphasis perhaps precisely because they were not easily understood, this is seen as undermining the authority of the Church. Not only the authorities feel this rather painfully, but the faithful, too, realize this instinctively. *And there lies the problem.*

This demands some *fundamental investigation* into the teaching function of the Church in moral matters. The precise role of the Church in the formulation and preaching of concrete moral norms must be explained to the faithful. The Church's task is to preserve in her life and teaching the Spirit of Christ, the knowledgeable awareness of man's dignity and the liberating force of the Gospel. From her understanding of the faith, and constantly referring to the evidence of the scriptures, she must explain and put into practice the commandment of love as it applies to man's life at every stage in his cultural development. However, she can do this only if she takes into account man's understanding of himself and of his world at every stage. Otherwise no *concrete* interpretation of moral law is possible at all. There can indeed be genuine obligations that are not universally valid, in the sense that they are not valid equally for all men in all ages.

There are striking examples of this in the exhortations of the primitive Church as we meet them in the readings at the Sunday Mass. The center of the primitive proclamation is the message of the Lord crucified, risen and glorified. The moral indications linked up with this message have a far-reaching importance as models.[10] They show the young communities and the individual Christian what concrete demands are made on them by a life of faith and love in an historical environment. Many of these exhortations and indications (e.g., concerning the *agape*) deal with an explanation and application of the command of love in the context of a life led in contemporary institutions that developed in the history of culture at that time. The personal rights (family, marriage, the position of woman) and the social institutions (slavery, capital punishment, military service) were *accepted* as facts but *by no means guaranteed as Christian*. On the contrary, the faithful are shown how they should approach these institutions in a new spirit, inspired by their faith in the risen Lord. And thus the seed is planted for a change from within, which, in the long run, could bring about a change in the institutions more effectively than a violent revolution would. Thus, for example, the proclamation of the Christian message stressed the meaning and exclusiveness of monogamy with growing effectiveness in the history of the West.[11]

[10] Cf. J. Blank, "Does the New Testament Provide Principles for Modern Moral Theology?" in *Concilium* 25 (1967), pp. 19f.

[11] Cf. D. S. Bailey, *Mann und Frau im christlichen Denken* (Stuttgart, 1963); O. Rousseau, "Divorce and Remarriage: East and West," in *Concilium* 24 (1967), pp. 113–38. See also the Documentation section in this volume.

The fact that this process was accompanied by one-sided stresses, exaggerations and subsequent correctives in the actual teaching and its proclamation is not an argument against what I have just said, but rather confirms it. That is why the biblical pattern must be supplemented by referring to typical developments in the norms that have taken place in the history of Christian morality. Examples can be found in social and economic ethics with regard to the treatment and function of property, the relation to the poor, the interpretation of the sentence "you will always have the poor with you", or the question of tribute or tax.[12]

Equally typical is the development that took place in sexual morality.[13] Augustine clearly developed his teaching on sex in reaction against the Manichaeans and Pelagians. That is why he accepts—not without leaning on the Stoic ideal of "apathy" —perfect self-control and complete sublimation in sexual intercourse through love, sanctified in the sacrament. And so, according to Augustine, sexual desire can only be tolerated because it is inevitable when sex has a function to fulfill—i.e., in procreation and the marital duty inside marriage. No one today will again preach this kind of dualism. Yet, *for his time* Augustine was a timely and in this sense "true" preacher of the Christian life according to the understanding of sex in that age. The same must be said of the sexual teaching at the peak of Scholasticism which tried in many ways to overcome this dualism of Augustine. For this purpose it linked the norms of its sexual ethics with Ulpian's doctrine of natural law which was then in vogue. Something similar happened to the sexual morality of the 17th and 18th centuries. In all cases the interpretation of Christian life in concrete issues—in other words, the question of what the consequences of the Christian conviction about the value, vocation and dignity of the human person are for one's actual moral behavior—depends in large measure on the his-

[12] Cf. J. T. Noonan, "Die Autoritätsbeweise in Fragen des Wuchers," in *Diakonia* 1 (1966), pp. 79–106.
[13] Cf. F. Böckle, "Sexualität u. sittliche Norm," in *St. Zeit.* 180 (Oct. 1967), pp. 247–67.

torically conditioned contemporary understanding of man in such matters. For instance, as long as there was no clear understanding of the biological process of procreation, the notions of the age would determine the so-called "metaphysical" interpretation of sexuality.

In practice the continuity and change in the teaching on marriage during the last fifty years stand out sharply against this background. *Casti connubii,* taken as a whole, was an urgently necessary and, in a way, open-minded statement. Over against a loud-voiced propaganda for far-reaching libertinism in sexual relationships, the saving force of monogamous marriage had to be put forth as a central point of the Christian proclamation. It was equally right to warn against an arbitrary and purely technical and calculating treatment of sexual relationships, since this contains, even today, considerable dangers to the personal love between the partners in marriage. At the same time, it was admitted that this does not *have to be* in every case. *The principle of selfless and true love,* which alone is the ultimate norm in the field of sexuality, *remained* and must remain the guiding principle. The application of this principle, however, leaves room for important modifications based on corresponding insights in the actual reality. This process of constantly applying anew the demands of a Christian existence to concrete life involves every believer, but, at the same time, is in many ways beyond him as an isolated individual. Here we touch on a totally new aspect of the necessity for an institutionalized seeking-after-truth in the Church where the norms for practical behavior are concerned. However, this exceeds the scope of our present subject.

2. *The Provisional Character of Morality*

The radical demands contained in the Sermon on the Mount have always been a difficulty in Christian preaching. The danger of Utopian dreams in the interpretation is equalled by the just as great danger of emasculating these demands by adjusting them to a bourgeois morality. Both sides have exchanged names in the course of the Church's history, but the problem has remained the same. Nor is it capable of a patent solution. Insofar as the Christian way of life is concerned, neither a two-level morality which binds the Christian middle class to the ten commandments and reserves the Sermon on the Mount for those who go in for a specified brand of sanctity, nor the Lutheran dialectic of the two kingdoms, nor a synthesis of nature and grace, of justice (natural law) and love, provides an adequate solution. "New Testament morality ultimately cannot be systematized, and for good reason." [14] This shows clearly in the difficulties about decisive issues of social ethics or political exhortation which comes out in the *Pastoral Constitution on the Church in the Modern World* of Vatican Council II.

In principle, therefore, we have here to create some understanding of the tension within salvation history to which Christian life is subject. Both the individual believer and the Church as the whole People of God under the New Covenant are on a pilgrimage from the beginning of salvation to its final fulfillment. During this pilgrimage the Church does not just stand over against the world but is herself first of all part of this world. There is a solidarity between the Church and the world, with all its confusion and all its needs. The Church is therefore also charged with being "the salt of the earth" and "the light of the world". She must constantly query the prevailing social morality in the light of the Gospel. But she must never give the impression that she is herself innocent of the situation of the world. "The situation in which the world finds itself is essentially the result of Christian achievement and Christian guilt" (W. Dirks). Nor can she behave as if she had a ready-made solution for every problem. We must shake off that narrow-minded morality which denies that there are objective obstructions and which has for every situation one solution that is allowed and one that is not allowed, a right solution and a wrong one. In many cases, particularly where consequential and therefore important decisions

[14] J. Blank, *art. cit.*, p. 13.

are concerned in the field of politics, economics and research, only a provisional answer can be found in the spirit of Christ, one answer among other possible ones.

In practice this can be illustrated with particular clarity in reference to the problems of war and peace. The worldwide importance of peace, as affecting the existence of all mankind, is obvious today. Ecclesiastical concern for peace, particularly shown by the popes of the last hundred years, has reached its highest point in *Pacem in terris,* the *Pastoral Constitution on the Church in the Modern World* and *Populorum progressio.* It has been significantly underlined by the personal commitment of the present pope, as shown in his speech to the United Nations, in the conflict over Vietnam and elsewhere. Yet, the subject of "peace" is practically never the topic of preaching, but this is certainly not because the importance of peace is underrated. The reason seems to be rather that the Church's appeals for peace are exclusively addressed to politicians and statesmen, not to the people as a whole. To make peace is the business of those who are "up there". The "little man" quite agrees with these appeals for peace by the Church, but he does not think himself involved since he sees no practical way of effectively contributing to peace. That is why he does not feel guilty in matters of war or a danger of war, except perhaps to the extent that he feels that "he has not prayed hard enough" for peace. Many priests share this state of mind, and so they avoid preaching about peace and limit themselves to an exhortation to prayer.

This attitude is disastrous, and a contributory cause to the lack of peace. This passive attitude of the people makes them fall victim to every kind of propaganda and to every deliberately manipulated prejudice in any conflict. We have to make people aware of the fact that the whole people shares in the responsibility for the situation in the world. Politicians are, in large measure, made by the people. They are dependent on public opinion. We must create in the broad masses of the people a climate of peace which gives the peace-minded politician a chance to make decisions that may be unpopular but are necessary for peace, and which prevents evil-minded or incapable politicians from indulging in activities that endanger peace.

Preaching about peace can therefore not be restricted to the question of a "just war". It cannot rest satisfied with a casuistic discussion of ways and means or with a purely theoretical explanation of what conditions are necessary before defense is allowed. The preacher should at least present conscientious objection as a genuine possible Christian decision in a situation which has changed since the atom bomb, and this particularly where a constructive peaceful service, such as help in developing countries, is allowed by the State as a substitute for military service (cf. *Constitution on the Church in the Modern World*, n. 78).

In the meantime, the main task of the preacher is to make people conscious of the fact that wars do not fall from heaven. Wars are not natural disasters. They are made by men. The sermon must explain that war guilt is difficult to localize, that it stretches much further and involves far more people than one would think on a superficial view. The sermon should name the causes of war: hunger and illness, economic misery, social injustice, exploitation and oppression, colonialism, racial discrimination, the selfishness of nations and particular power groups, philosophical and ideological barriers and prejudices, and, lastly, ambition and lust for power. To collaborate actively in the elimination of these causes is everybody's business. To withdraw from any such collaboration makes one guilty of lack of peace in the world. The opportunities for commitment are varied and depend on the individual. They stretch from modestly contributing to the creation of a peace-minded public opinion within one's immediate environment, to practical service for peace (Peace Corps, aid to developing countries) and acceptance of political responsibility up to the point of bloody or unbloody witness (political protest, refusal to cooperate with a manifestly unjust government to one's personal disadvantage, and so on). There are obviously many kinds and many degrees of guilt in these matters. It does not *start* with a war crime. For example, it should be obvious to any Christian that to reject, on principle, aid to developing countries or some other form of responsibility for people of another nationality than one's own is altogether irreconcilable with the Christian faith.

Further, it should be shown that war has assumed a totally new quality in this atomic age. The concrete possibility of an atomic war with millions of dead will exist as long as there are hostile power blocs and national sovereignty remains absolute, and the danger will disappear only when mankind is united. The creation of world peace puts all other political problems, such as questions of boundaries between particular nations and problems of national minorities or political (and denominational!) power groups with private interests, into the shade, or, rather, subordinates them to the overriding program of world peace, and so frequently gives them another slant. For example, individual political decisions at a political election must be made in the light of world peace. World peace demands from everyone great sacrifices, renouncements and a readiness to compromise.

Finally, the preacher must show both the interdependence and the distinction between world peace and the peace of Christ. Political peace should not be understood as a kind of Pelagian self-redemption. But this does not allow the Christian to emigrate from the world. The peace of Christ may reach its fulfillment only in the future, but it is already operative in the present. The mere statement of God's promise of salvation (or peace) necessarily implies a command. The peace of Christ which is bestowed on redeemed man demands that it be worked out within the scope of this world. Political world peace is not identical with God's peace, but is closely intertwined with it.

3. No More Individualistic Morality

For several reasons Catholic moral theology has been predominantly individualistic for a long time. One of them is that the canon which demands that the penitent must declare all his grave sins in kind and number (DS 1707) forced moral theology to overconcentrate on the field of the individual conscience. This was encouraged by the prevailing tendency of an individualistic culture. Within the Churches of the Reformation there has been a parallel development. Just as in pietism one prayed for God's grace for the individual, so the question among Catholics was how far the individual could go without endangering his salvation by mortal sin. This does not mean that the Churches were wholly unconcerned in earlier days about social or political issues, but moral theology without any doubt concentrated on the individual's attitude toward God, himself and his neighbor. This fell definitely short of the Christian task to contribute to the shaping and development of a social morality. This is precisely the problem we touched on before in mentioning our responsibility for peace in connection with preaching. Therefore Christians must be made far more aware of their responsibility for the shaping of our social and political life. I must stress that I am not referring to an individual crusade of the good Christian, nor to an attempt to convert the wicked world. It is much more a matter of a committed and constructive cooperation of Christians in finding a solution to burning issues thrown up by economics, science and technology. All Christians must be informed about them, and those who have the ability should be actively involved in them.

In principle, therefore, the sermon must constantly show that, and how, the Gospel message is a message of salvation for the world, a social message in the best sense of the word. This does not make the Bible an expression of collectivist thought. The witness of the Bible cannot be wholly secured for any social theory. Neither the individualist nor the collectivist can harness the Bible to his bandwagon. This would seem obvious when we see that neither individualism nor collectivism leaves room for a theocracy. It is nevertheless true that the message of salvation is linked with the community in both the Old and the New Testaments. Salvation history is the history of the People of God, which is extended in the new covenant to the whole family of mankind.

I pointed out above how this fact came out in the preaching of the early Church. There was no proclamation of a political program in the name of Christ, but by preaching the equal value and dignity of all men "in Christ" and making this the basis of brotherly love, a new criterion and a powerful stimulus were given for the gradual transformation of society. That Christians themselves only too often failed to take this criterion seriously, or that the concrete social consequences of this were misunderstood, makes one understand the often bitter reproaches made by atheists, but does not alter the fact that the liberating force of the Gospel has persisted with growing intensity. So far no philosophy has succeeded in providing positive proof for the eternal and enduring value of the human person. Only the revelation that the infinite God infinitely loves the individual person guarantees the Christian's recognition of man's dignity. This is a treasure which implies heavy responsibility and demands social and political involvement.

In practice these problems make heavy demands on the preacher. The fact that Christian teaching offers no ready-made solutions for our social problems demands restraint. Christ's spirit and message leave room for several solutions in many concrete cases. On the other hand, the preacher cannot avoid the issue because it is difficult. He should frankly admit that there can be a difference of opinion in practice about a particular point. He should try the harder to throw light on the various possibilities with the help of basic Christian principles and so provide a few basic points along which a decision might be reached. And while he should not put forth his own view as absolute and conclusive, why should he not occasionally bear personal witness before the community? He may not be able to prove it fully, but it can be a genuine witness based on his conviction, his sense of faith. If in so doing he makes himself the advocate of the poor and the weak, who will blame him? Often it will be enough to reveal a hidden need or to point firmly to a well-known disease in the social body, and to link this with a few practical suggestions and an urgent call for help. Is *Populorum progressio* not the best illustration of that? Here the magisterium at its highest level developed a new style which shows the preacher *the way from doctrinal teaching to witness.*

Apart from what we might call typical problems of social morality, today there is also a whole series of issues which until now were mainly approached from an individualistic angle and so could hardly provide a convincing answer. An example is the question of genetic manipulations. This much-discussed problem can of course be treated today as a matter of what an individual is allowed to do as such—in other words, whether a given researcher is allowed to make this or that experiment. But such questions can hardly be answered satisfactorily without referring to all kind of presuppositions that are far from clear in themselves. Such an answer would in no way alter or stop altogether the course of events. But the whole problem can also be viewed from the angle of social morality. One may ask, for instance, under what conditions these so-called manufacturers of man can reach the desired effect at all? The practical execution of their planning may require such vast changes in the social substructures that success seems possible only at the cost of individual freedom (as in a dictatorship).

With all this we are not any the wiser about the lawfulness of an individual intervention, but at least it shows anyone concerned with this that it is not enough for such problems to proceed from the mere technical possibility and that the universally human and social implications of all concerned must be very carefully taken into consideration. Here we have an important function for theology and the preaching of theology: it is *not* so much its task to look at *concrete individual actions* (which it can practically never judge adequately), as it is to keep a sharp eye on the universally human consequences of what may be an alluring hypothesis. We should leave the judgment about the individual steps and possibilities in this process to the alert conscience of the properly informed professionals.

This is far from all that could be said about this problem of genetic manipulation. The question was only put by way of illustrating the decisive fact that as Christians we should not lose ourselves in discussions about details that are not connected with faith. Instead of that, we should use every opportunity to discuss the social aspects of every question, frankly and honestly, with all men of goodwill. We would then undoubtedly achieve more, and here the preacher should make a definite contribution.

Helmut Gollwitzer/*Berlin, W. Germany*

Reconciliation: Ideal or Reality?

I

THE CHRISTIAN CONCEPT OF RECONCILIATION

The value and the real core of the Christian message are sources of much dispute between Christians and non-Christians, believers and non-believers. Yet, despite these disagreements, there is surprising unanimity on one point: Christians are supposed to be men of reconciliation. Believers, non-believers and theologians will agree that if a man calls himself a Christian, other men have a right to expect that he will dedicate himself to promoting reconciliation among men.

Reconciliation means that a chasm is bridged, that a dispute is settled. Quarreling parties are led from opposition to agreement and collaboration. Everyone agrees that the realization of such harmony must be the goal of Christian effort. There is also unanimous agreement that this obligation of the Christian embraces *all* men; it does not apply to some specific group. When a Christian community restricts its work of reconciliation to a small circle and excludes others, it betrays its basic nature.

The unanimous agreement on this aspect of Christianity is independent of people's acceptance or rejection of it. Whether they approve or disapprove, they accept this as the obligation of a real Christian. For Nietzsche, it is a reason for criticizing Christianity. For Fascism, it is a reason for persecuting Chris-

81

tianity. Modern trends in theological thought[1] focus on this as the core of the Christian message; integrating the Christian message around this idea, they use it as the criterion for determining the essential elements in Christian tradition and its authentic lines of development.

To all appearances it would seem that this core concept is lofty and worthy of approval. It is not so self-evident, however, when we come up against the criticisms of someone like Nietzsche who was especially critical of the universality which is an intrinsic note in the Christian concept of love. In reality, both the value and the practicability of reconciliation, as a Christian ideal, are disputed and disputable; they must be defended on sound grounds.

In contrast to the Christian concept of universal reconciliation, Nietzsche upheld the cultivation of an elite. In contrast to the Christian call to serve the cause of reconciliation, Lenin summoned the proletariat to irreconcilable warfare and revolution. Moltke's assertion that eternal peace is a dream (and not such a great dream either) challenges the Christian ideal of a human race guided by the principle of reconciliation. Once we leave the realm of pious ideas and enter the real world, a host of questions arise over this Christian ideal.

It may be true enough that it is nice to see quarrels patched up once in a while. But does this justify making reconciliation the guiding principle of life, as Christianity does? Aren't there certain limits beyond which reconciliation cannot and should not be sought? Should it be really universal in scope? Aren't there limits set by racial differences, inferiority and the weight of guilty wrongdoing? When the Bolsheviks announced the opening of a new era "to all men" in 1917, it was not directed to "all" men in the same spirit. It was a friendly greeting to the oppressed and a threat to their oppressors. When Christianity

---

[1] "Modern" might well be put in quotation marks. The so-called modern trends in theology are now over two hundred years old, a venerable age indeed. Somehow its proponents manage to keep it looking young.

sounds its unrestricted call to "all men",[2] it evokes cries of protest from the racial, political, religious and moral differences among men, for they are threatened by this call. The reasons justifying these differences serve to cast a cloud over the practicability and even the desirability of the Christian ideal, at least in the eyes of many.

The practicability of this ideal also casts doubts on its merits. Can it truly be realized? Does it not face insuperable obstacles and difficulties? What chance does it have in the real world? Who has the power to make it a reality? Who is joyous enough to carry it through (for the real Christian must be joyous in carrying it out, not reluctant and grumbling)? Efforts at effecting reconciliation must spring from an irrepressible joy in the task.

The command to be a man promoting reconciliation may seem self-evident. Everyone may agree that reconciliation is better than quarreling. We may be strongly attracted by the Utopian dream of a world at peace. But all this does not erase the gap between the real world in which I live and the dream world to which I am summoned. I am enmeshed in a world where reconciliation is not a reality. If I am to go about the task of reconciliation joyfully, I must be free of these entanglements. As Luther points out, the injunction of the commandment does not provide the living conditions that are required to ensure its fulfillment.

Thus the validity and the practicability of the Christian principle of reconciliation cannot be proved on the basis of the Word itself or the ideal it proposes; nor, to be sure, can it be proved by pointing to the present social order. We must look elsewhere.

[2] One must not restrict the meaning of "panti tō laō" (Lk. 2, 10) to "homines bonae voluntatis" by mistranslating Luke 2, 14.

II

THE REAL BASIS OF THIS COMMANDMENT

When we seek to discover the basis and the motive force of this commandment of reconciliation, we are simply asking why it is so *necessary*. Why is it the distinctive Christian commandment, the one which integrates all the other commandments? From where does it derive its overwhelming importance over against all other commandments, ideals and interests? Whence this affirmation and approval of all things human that find expression in it?

These questions bring us to the connection between dogma and ethics. If the question cannot be answered on purely ethical grounds, then any attempt to reduce the Christian message to ethics and to separate Christian ethics from dogma is doomed to failure. Since the Enlightenment, people have been trying to do this in a variety of ways, and the attempt is still going on. Their hope is to be able to salvage the kernel of the Christian message from the harsh attacks of the Enlightenment. This kernel would survive demythologization and would not presume an act of faith. It would be immediately evident, and it could be correlated to our real life without further ado.

My thesis, however, is that we cannot keep one without the other. We cannot have ethics without dogma, the commandment of reconciliation without the reconciliation-event of which dogma speaks. Separated from the event described in the dogma of reconciliation, the commandment of reconciliation could prove worthy for a while, but it would eventually fade out. It would then end up as a purely philanthropic ideal without a real driving force, or its scope would be restricted to something less than all men; it would seem only right to exclude some people (cf. Mt. 5, 46).

The commandment of reconciliation derives its force from its roots in the dogma of reconciliation. From there it derives its urgency and its inevitability, its unlimited scope and universality, its meaningfulness and its practicability.

For the New Testament, the indissoluble connection between dogma and commandment is indisputable. The reconciliation between God and man, effected by Jesus Christ, is the explicit and implicit basis for the commandment of reconciliation. Having introduced this historical note, we can now inquire after the objective, internal connection between them. And we might well start by seeing what the New Testament and Christian tradition have to say about it.

Even before we introduce the dogma of reconciliation into the picture, we find that the notion of a reconciliation between God and man says certain things about the human condition:

1. Mankind (each and every man) has a relationship not only with the world (the sum total of creatures) and with other men, but also with someone else. This relationship runs vertical to all other relationships. It is a real relationship that is far different from interhuman relationships.

2. This relationship embraces all the other relationships in which man is involved. It is the first, the last, and the support of all these relationships. In other words, without this there would be no other relationships; it passes irrevocable judgment on all the relationships of human life.

3. This vertical relationship is shared by all men and all created beings. It sets them all off as "the world" over against one who is not "the world"; it sets creation over against the creator.

4. This relationship can change, without thereby being dissolved. It is, in short, a relationship in history. It can be one of peace or one of strife. Thus for man, the lesser partner in the relationship, it can be life or death, meaningfulness or senselessness, a claim to existence or loss of this claim.

III

THEOLOGICAL ASPECTS OF THIS COMMANDMENT

Presuming that the commandment of reconciliation is rooted in the dogmatic reality of reconciliation, can we show that it is as necessary as we have made it out to be? Let us spell out some of the basic theological aspects involved.

1. *God's Initiative*

Rooted in the reconciliation-event, the commandment of reconciliation is a call to action, but our action stems from a prior state of receptivity. Man does not go into action from a state of rest; he reacts to an initiative from without. He is summoned to carry on a process that is already under way, a process that is to be carried further by him. Thus it challenges the notion of quietism, which springs from a misunderstanding of Luther's doctrine of justification and stresses the passive role of man in the reception of grace. As Adolf Schlatter put it: "Giving is more blessed than receiving, and service is the aim of grace." This is certainly true insofar as the doctrine of reconciliation is concerned.

But this giving presupposes a prior receiving. We can only give after we have received. That is an obvious but irrevocable stipulation on human existence. It becomes particularly pointed in our present connection, for the giving is blessed only when it proceeds from a condition of wealth; only then can the giver be unconcerned about himself. When Jesus said, "Give to everyone who asks of you", there was behind his words an unspoken presupposition that we have an inexhaustible store of riches at our disposal.

To be inexhaustibly rich, however, one would have to have an inexhaustible store of wealth. Of ourselves we are not even rich, much less inexhaustibly rich. So Jesus' command goes beyond our capabilities. It is rooted in the fact that the apostles, as men reconciled and united with God, can avail themselves of an inexhaustible store of riches. Without God man is not rich, so purely ethical considerations must involve an evaluation of the relative worth of various interests.

This is the radical difference between Jesus' golden rule ("Do unto others as you would have them do unto you") and the golden rule as formulated negatively ("Don't do to others what you don't want done to you"). Penal laws can back up the latter formulation; only the Gospel can support Jesus' formula. Our ability to give stems from the fact we have received; our work of reconciling stems from the fact of our own reconciliation.

2. God's Reconciliation Is Irresistible

God's work of reconciliation turns poverty into wealth; it also turns resignation into confident trust. The realities of life dampen our high-minded ideals and our desire to be men of reconciliation. Problems and difficulties change us from idealists into realists; we resign ourselves to the way things are. Life tells us to come to terms with the limited nature of our possessions and our capabilities and to resign ourselves to the limits imposed on our goodwill by the folly and wickedness of others.

The reconciliation-event makes it even clearer that we ourselves cannot be relied on to bring the world to reconciliation; it is beyond our power. The reconciliation-event turns our resignation toward the world into despair over ourselves. But it is a despair filled with confidence; it is, in Luther's words, "desperatio fiducialis", for the message of reconciliation tells us that divine reconciliation wins out over us and despite us. It does not find in us a suitable disposition, nor does it rely on this. It is the *irresistible* action of God's creative Word. This fact is symbolized in the Virgin Birth (Christ is born in the dead of night, while men sleep) and it is brought out in the resurrection (Christ is raised without men being aware of it).

The irresistible nature of God's reconciliatory activity is a clarion call to us; it offers us comfort and encouragement in our own work of reconciling men. Without this heritage to back us up, we would carefully weigh our relative strength and weakness against the forces opposing us; we would falter at the limits of our own potentialities. Rooted in God's work of reconciliation, our work of reconciliation acquires new perspectives, new depths of courage and new wellsprings of hope. We no longer pin our hopes on some spark of goodness left in man; instead, *on behalf of* all men, we put our hope in the creative goodness of God and dare to undertake the work of reconciliation.

3. *Christ: Reconciliation Personified*

Reconciliation means that people, once separated, are brought together. In the work of reconciliation we help people to bridge the differences between them. We help them to look each other in the eye, to treat each other as brothers and to bear responsibility for each other's needs. But why do they have real claims on each other? From where does the unity of mankind take on ethical relevance? The common origin of the species is not sufficient to serve as the basis for brotherhood; it can produce intra-species aggression as well as communication.

Jesus Christ does more than bid men to act *as if* they were brothers; "he himself *is* our peace" (Eph. 2, 14). In his person he is our reconciliation. In his life and activity God and man are brought together and indissolubly united, and so are *man and man*. In our work of reconciliation we are not trying to realize something that is not yet a reality; we are actually trying to relate ourselves to something that has already been made a reality by Christ. Our work of reconciliation is not a counter-offensive against reality; instead, man's non-reconciliatory actions are an attack on the reconciliation that is already a reality.

4. *A Reconciliation with No Limits*

Our reconciliation is embodied and made incarnate in Jesus Christ; he is our reconciliation. This tells us that reconciliation is a reality which affects the real life of man in its every aspect. Reconciliation cannot be reduced to vague, spiritualistic terms; *it cannot be interpreted too materialistically.*

Reconciliation is not just a state of mind, an interpersonal encounter on the purely intellectual, religious or private level without social implications or repercussions. The Christian's work of reconciliation, rooted in God's work of reconciliation, is not infected with Docetist haughtiness. It approaches man where he is, facing the conflicts that exist and trying to eliminate the causes of alienation.

Now that the chasm between God and man has been truly bridged, the Christian cannot regard any chasm as insuperable. In his work of reconciliation he boldly confronts all sources of conflict—material, political, economic, social and racial. In view of God's work of reconciliation, man makes bold to promote reconciliation on any and every level—without restriction or reservation.

5. *Reconciliation: A Drive toward Truth*

God's work of reconciliation does not entail covering up the truth; it lays bare the truth. Judgment is not abdicated; it is given its full and proper scope. Thanks to God's work of reconciliation, man's work of reconciliation is encouraged to seek truth, to stand up against unrighteousness, and to uncover guilty behavior. Now reconciliation does not always mean the "golden mean"; on a given occasion, it can take sides in a dispute and cast the deciding vote.

While Christian reconciliation never closes its heart to people, it may be obdurate on a given issue. Its purpose, of course, is to promote brotherly collaboration among men in *God's* world, to effect the fulfillment of God's plan for his creation. This does not preclude or pre-determine the question of methods, but it does mean that every method and every manner of action must be tested by certain questions: Does it spring from a belief in the reality of reconciliation? Does it seek to realize reconciliation? [3]

IV

THE RELATIONSHIP BETWEEN DOGMA AND COMMANDMENT

How can God's activity find echoes in our activity? How can our activity acquire some of the elements to be found in God's

[3] This brings up the old question: To what extent can force be used in the service of reconciliation?

work—inexhaustibility, hope, universality, orientation to reality and truth? According to the New Testament, this is effected through the Word, as an instrument of the Spirit, and through faith which accepts this Word. In pointing out that our work of reconciliation derives from God's work of reconciliation, we have spelled out the significance of *faith* for our *activity,* our *works.* Herein lies the only genuine connection between dogma and ethics.

Taken in isolation, the commandment itself loses its full dimensions. Its content and its root source are watered down, so that it becomes merely a matter of purely human possibilities. But when it is heard with the ear of faith, when it is heard as the "form of the Gospel" (Karl Barth), as a way of encountering God's reconciliation-event, then it awakens the joyous hope of moving step by step beyond purely human possibilities.

Christian life is the life of a man who has been reconciled to God and who now works for man's reconciliation. That is the connection between dogma and commandment, and it should be underlined. It is the basis for *judging* the Christian individual and the Christian community.

Church history, too, is the story of a continuing chasm between dogma and commandment. Interhuman rifts have not been overcome; social conflicts have not been resolved. Christian activity for reconciliation has not turned reconciliation into a reality on earth. The universal brotherhood of man has been reduced to the brotherhood of believers; it has been defined on religious grounds. A variety of theological theories have been advanced to justify leaving the world unchanged, and they have only hardened the existing lines of separation. Indeed, new lines of separation have been added.

By separating dogma from commandment, Christians paved the way for those humanists who separated commandment from dogma. The dogma lost its power, and the commandment was turned into a vague ideal. To the shame of Christians, the vague humanist ideal often had more influence on real action than did the Christian dogma. Those who denigrated the law often put the adherents of the Gospel to shame.

What we say about the relevance of dogma for practical action must be verified in Christian practice. Without this verification, it looks like a Christian attempt at one-upmanship over the humanists. Only when Christian behavior eliminates the chasm between dogma and action can we make a forceful case for their interconnection before the bar of humanism.

Domingo Castagna/*Buenos Aires, Argentina*

Should the Laity Preach Today?

The sense of the term "preaching", as applied to today's actual pastoral practice, has to be limited by the following negative section of Canon Law: "All those who are not clerics, even if they be religious, are forbidden to preach in church" (CCL, Canon 1342, §2).

1. *The Historical Background*

In the course of Church history it can be proved that episcopal authority has conferred the preaching ministry on laymen. From the proclamation of the apostolic kerygma to the emergence of a theologically more fully developed form of preaching, we find that the principal activity is in the hands of the apostles and their successors but with the immediate collaboration of the other members of the hierarchy and of laymen. The organization of the clergy into its distinct grades and a narrow concept of hierarchy gave rise to a sort of exclusiveness in the ministry of preaching. The increasingly intensive formation of the clergy was a justification for this exclusiveness. Theology itself has, right up to our own day, been a clerical preserve. For this reason, those responsible for the care of the community have found themselves compelled to reserve the ministry of preaching almost exclusively

92

to priests or experienced clerics. Nonetheless, the right to preach was also granted to laymen, though to a very limited extent; such preaching was, to begin with, only in the form of exhortation, but later, in response to new needs arising in Christian communities, it took the form of apologetics.

2. Preaching and Ecclesial Ministry

In order to reach a valid conclusion we must risk a definition of preaching in its narrowest sense. We understand the term as meaning the exercise of the apostolic magisterium to transmit the faith. Preaching, considered as the solemn and divinely authorized proclamation of God's revelation, belongs therefore to the episcopal college. The magisterium of this college is, in the field proper to it, infallible, and for that reason cannot be delegated. Nonetheless, the college of bishops can give a share, albeit a totally subordinate one, in its own mission to other members of the Church; today it does so to priests and deacons.

In order to give full value to the ecclesial ministry and to the importance of the episcopal college in the supreme exercise of that ministry, we have to keep in view the organic nature of the Church as a whole. The plenitude of ecclesial powers that belonged to the apostles as heads is essential for the understanding of what the Church is. Through the apostles and their successors, Christ exercises his dominion over the whole ecclesial assembly. The Lord is the prophet who makes his people a prophetic people, the priest who makes it priestly, the king who makes it royal. The ministerial priesthood, existing in its fullness in the apostles, serves the community as a sacramental instrument through which Christ himself provides those means that establish and build up his people.

In virtue of that same organic nature of the Church, each member of the body shares in all the concerns of the head and is capable of executing his orders. The members of the Church of Christ are ministers of the proclamation of the mystery of their head in order to call men to conversion by the obedience of faith.

3. *The Charisms as a Constituent Element of the Church*

Side by side with the essential structure of the Church, concerning which Vatican Council II spoke at length in its *Constitution on the Church,* there exists another reality that is also a constituent of the mystery of the Church—namely, the charisms. These free gifts, ordered to the building up of the kingdom of God, are independent of any ecclesiastical structure; they are born of the free movement of the Holy Spirit. Immaturity of faith has been the obstacle to the emergence of these charisms in the members of the Church.

In virtue of the charisms, the Holy Spirit can use any member whatsoever of the Church as an instrument with which to intervene in and give light to human lives. It is difficult to be unaware of the presence, in potency or in act, of special charisms in the baptized.

4. *The Ecclesial Nature of the Layman*

There does exist among the members of the Church a distinction that does not harm but rather builds up her unity—namely, the distinction between clerics, religious and laity. We shall deal only with the last two, since the question that concerns clerics has been posed with reference to them. By "layman" we mean a fully initiated Christian—that is, one who has received the sacraments of baptism and confirmation. Through baptism he receives the grace of being incorporated into the Church, of being the Church; through confirmation he receives the grace of being so incorporated perfectly. Karl Rahner affirms that the Church is "the historical and social setting of the grace of Christ in the world", and he attributes the same reality to every baptized person. This grace of Christ, which is the Church as a whole, calls men to salvation and effectively saves them. The conciliar *Constitution on the Church* discusses the ecclesial nature of the layman, asserting the reality of his status as a member of God's people and as a sharer in the very salvific mission of the whole Church. Rahner lucidly develops the same truth, stating that baptismal grace transforms man "into an actively functioning unit within this community, someone who shares in the basic functions of this community".

What dogmatic objection can therefore be found to exclude the laity from a genuine sharing in the apostolic ministry of the Word? The present juridical prohibition has behind it a disciplinary decision of the Church; it can therefore be modified the moment that such a modification is demanded by the needs of the ecclesial community.

5. *The Demands of the Present Moment*

Solid evidence indicates the present urgency of a revision of the negative canonical legislation on this topic and the reestablishment of a genuine participation by the layman in the apostolic ministry of preaching.

The sense of the Church, insistently brought home to the laity in various pontifical documents of this century—particularly those concerned with promoting the Catholic Action movement —has created an authentic climate of renewal with which the whole lay intervention, authorized or commissioned by the episcopal hierarchy, in the field of catechetics and missions has been entirely consonant. But the current evolution of pastoral practice seems to us to demand something more.

All the structures of the Church are penetrated by the urgency of the need for evangelization. All the members of the Church without exception are acquiring a clearer awareness of their salvific mission, and those traditionally classed as "non-hierarchy" are driven to a mature assumption of the responsibility that belongs to them in the proclamation of the Gospel.

The Council exhorts the laity to share in pastoral work and responsibility to the full extent of their capacity or of the charisms which they have received. The presence of the layman at pastoral conferences and the formation he is undergoing by reason of his study, prayer and apostolic activity shows us that the layman is preparing himself for fuller participation in important tasks that have, up to the present moment, been entrusted exclusively to the clergy. The liturgical renewal, by granting to laymen certain ministerial functions in the liturgy, presupposes the layman's fundamental capability. On the other hand, the contemporary phenomenon of the shortage of clergy, particularly in the foreign missions and in Latin America, poses a serious dilemma. If the sharing by laymen in the ministry of preaching remains totally prohibited, we run the risk of leaving innumerable men without Christian life; in the case of Latin America, this means genuine communities of baptized persons who are in danger of total loss of faith. The bishops of our dioceses of the interior—I have Argentina specifically in mind—have to live in a permanent state of mission activity if they want their pastoral action to bear any certain fruit. But on every single occasion they can see that three or four days of mission work are not sufficient, and they feel an unceasing concern about the state of abandonment in which these Christians will remain, without anyone to preside over them and to call them together. There already exist magnificent forerunners of an effort to provide for these priestless communities. The Rural Movement and the Rural Missions have achieved a great deal, but the urgent needs of the Church demand a more radical solution, the confiding of a certain hierarchical mission to responsible laymen established in permanent posts.

6. *Two Conclusions*

In answer to the title of this article, I give two conclusions. The layman *should* preach, in the broad sense of the word, proclaiming by his consciously ecclesial life the kerygma of salvation, which is the principal object of the ministry of preaching. Within this consciously ecclesial life we should also include preaching by the word, in conformity with the declarations of the Council. The layman *can* preach, in the restricted sense of the term, because he is a subject capable of sharing in the exercise of the apostolic magisterium.

7. Psychological Preparation

The putting into practice of any plan for preaching by laymen has a number of obstacles to overcome.[1] As is the case with every important reform in the Church, there will be need of a serious psychological preparation within Christian communities. Our people are still too "clericalized" to be able to take without resentment the mission of another baptized person exercising so sacred a ministry. Very regrettably, there has been a quite false opposition set up between the lay and the sacred, with the former considered as profane. A great deal of hard work will have to be done in the Church to clear men's minds of such prejudices.

Another difficulty is the training of the men to be appointed. The movement of pastoral renewal is tending to create adult communities within which suitable subjects will spontaneously come

[1] For further reading on the subject, the reader is referred to the following sources: K. Delahaye, "Laienpredigt," in *Lexikon f. Th. u. K.* (Freiburg, ²1961), cols. 741–48 (see also the bibliography appended thereto); G. Philips, *Der Laie in der Kirche* (Salzburg, 1955), pp. 127–48; Yves Congar, *Lay People in the Church* (London, 1965); H. Heimerl, *Kirche, Klerus und Laien* (Vienna, 1961), pp. 125–32; for literature on individual historical questions (Eastern Church, Waldensians, Luther, etc.), cf. K. Delahaye, *loc. cit.;* Th. Maertens in *Paroisse et Liturgie* 42 (1960), pp. 499–503; J. B. Schneyer, "Die Laienpredigt im Mittelalter," in *Münchener theologischer Zeitschrift* 18 (1967), pp. 205–18. With the end of the Council the whole question now needs a fresh review in view of the numerous relevant conciliar decisions and statements: the common priesthood of all believers, the teaching on charisms, the Church as the "People of God", the relationship between clergy and laity, the nature of the lay function in the Church, etc. A fresh examination of this whole question that would supplement and correct earlier work is still required.

forward. Nonetheless, under the actual circumstances of today, what will be needed is the creation of effective means for the immediate training of candidates. The decision to establish the diaconate as a permanent order is a provisional, not a definitive solution. Some baptized men could have a vocation of service to the community without needing for that service a distinct hierarchical ordination. This is the case of those called to exercise the ministry of preaching in the Church.

Leo Waltermann/*Cologne, W. Germany*

Preaching on the Radio

P reaching on the radio has gone on for decades. The expansion of the airwaves and the increased listening audience led people to expect an increased impact from what is said over those airwaves. Yet, at the same time, we have discovered somewhat belatedly that the broadcasting microphone has its own peculiar nature. It forces us not only to reexamine the form of what is said (the delivery), but also to alter its content. Both the "how" and the "what" come into question.

We cannot approach the radio microphone with the techniques of pulpit preaching, as if we were addressing a liturgical assembly, nor can the lessons of broadcasting be applied unreservedly to pulpit preaching. Having made these reservations, we still can say that the possible relevance of these two types of preaching for each other is a complex and many-sided question. The experiences of different people are varied and contradictory, and this holds true for the experiences of a given individual as well. There are no cut-and-dried formulas, and any attempt to devise them ends up in trite generalizations ("Be concrete!") or unserviceable prohibitions ("Don't get emotional!"). Nevertheless, our experiences with broadcast preaching may provide some valuable lessons for the pulpit preacher.

I

THE RADIO AS A PULPIT

Broadcasting Religious Programs

The experiences discussed here are not those of a radio preacher but of a radio editor who handles religious and theological programming for a community station. The station is not owned by the government or by a private enterprise. Regulated by certain basic legal prescriptions, it is entirely autonomous in its programming.[1] Its agents have sole and exclusive responsibility for all its programs. This does not infringe on the personal responsibility of contributors (e.g., preachers, authors, etc.), but even in its religious programs the station is not a technical tool for official Church pronouncements. Its religious programming involves more than sermon hours, for it includes news reports, commentaries, teaching programs and theological discussions.

The job in question involves working with theologians, religious writers and religious topics. It includes the general areas of theology, religion and Church, which form one general category within the station's overall programming ("symphony and opera" being another sample category). Thus the station's programming does not serve as an instrument of the institutional Church or as her broadcasting mouthpiece. The editorial work covers the general category of religion, and it is not restricted to any particular Church. Here, however, I shall discuss my experiences with an eye on Catholic preaching.

Preparing Programs and Sharing Experiences

The experiences mentioned here are not those of a single individual. Editors of various programming departments at the

---

[1] Legislation on broadcasting falls under the competence of the provincial parliaments, and the basic legal guidelines are similar for all radio stations. The legislation governing this particular station (Gesetz über den Westdeutschen Rundfunk, Köln, May 25, 1954) sets down the general constitutional guidelines within which the station is to operate. It must, for example, respect the moral and religious convictions of its listeners, promote peace and social justice, uphold democratic freedoms and truth, and avoid becoming the tool of special-interest groups (n. 4).

same station have compared notes over the years, as have editors of identical departments at different stations. There have also been workshops and editorial conferences with contributors and competent ecclesiastical organs.

The Cologne station, for example, has held regular conferences for contributors to its regular religious programs. A contributor who was making his first appearance on the air was often invited to one- or two-day sessions, where his text was examined and trial runs were made. Contributors to certain series were often invited back to hear the programs of a given period once again, and to offer their criticisms.

Later, modifications were introduced into this setup. Preachers over a six-month period, competent ecclesiastical representatives and station editors would meet weeks ahead of time to discuss the topics under consideration. Talks were written up and exchanged among the contributors so that they might interchange critical comments. Another two-day editorial conference took place later.

Members of these conferences were almost unanimous in their agreement that comparable preparatory procedures should be part and parcel of seminary training, and that similar meetings between priest and laity would benefit parochial preaching. Yet, despite their favorable reaction to these meetings, they saw no immediate possibility of introducing such procedures into their own particular work environment. Nor did the final broadcast product seem to measure up to the effort, money and enthusiasm invested in its preparation. The *modus operandi* used by the competent ecclesiastical authorities in selecting preachers may have been responsible for this, at least to some extent. Hopefully, the procedure has been used in some parochial communities and made some contribution to the betterment of parish preaching.

Using Public-Opinion Research

Comments from listeners, even those concerning sermon hours, can be used to best advantage when they are corroborated by data from other sources. Scientific public-opinion research can provide important data on broad items (sociological breakdown of listening audience, audience size at specific times of day or year, etc.) and on narrower questions (audience for a particular program, etc.). Yet such research has been used all too little in this connection.

For reasons that are not entirely satisfactory, religious programming is usually excluded from such public-opinion research. These programs only crop up in general surveys of audience listening habits. To this day such programs seem to be part of a medieval environment; they are excluded from the scope of public-opinion research, and they do not enter into comparisons with other types of programming.

The first results of a study begun in 1967 clearly indicate that the sociological picture is hardly in accord with the hopes and projections of those who are involved in these religious programs.[2] It was hoped that liturgical programs would reach an audience which can no longer be reached within the doors of the Church. But preachers and official representatives of the Church must come to realize that we cannot project the data of our own private world into the broad realm of social behavior; the impressions picked up from our own narrow environment must be examined and tested critically before they are taken as truly representative. It is a fact, for example, that in recent years the

[2] Consider this example. A five-minute sermonette is broadcast three times each weekday morning, at 5:55, 6:55 and 8:35. Its regular audience is very small—44% have never heard it, 33% have seldom heard it. Almost all its listeners are people interested in the programs that follow or precede it. Thus there is no hard-core listening audience that turns on the radio to listen to this show specifically. The program reaches churchgoers and non-churchgoers indiscriminately. The size of the listening audience has dropped in recent years—by one-third since 1964—for the two later time slots. About 10% of the total radio audience listen to the 5:55 broadcast—that means about 1.1 million listeners. But not all these listeners are interested in this particular program. They listen to the programs before and after, and do not bother to shut off the radio in between. Characteristic criticisms of the program are that it is "out of contact with reality", that it is "far-fetched", that it pretends to have "a solution for everything", and that it "points an accusing finger" at the audience.

listening audience for a Sunday or feast day broadcast is 50%
less than the audience for comparable non-liturgical and even
non-religious broadcasts.[3]

II

THE WORLD OF THE MICROPHONE

A Public Composed of Individuals

The radio preacher does not address a congregation; he ad-
dresses the public. Even his churchgoing audience, for whom
"congregation" is a social reality that extends beyond the liturgical assembly, hears his talk as members of the public and not
as members of this congregation. In contrast to other types of
listeners, the radio audience is a public of separate individuals
rather than some type of group.

The microphone is a means of multiplying oneself, and its
broad effectiveness is one clear reason for its zealous use. But in
using it we must remember that it is geared to a public composed
of single individuals. Objectivity, discretion, honesty and the
avoidance of emotionalism are not simply questions of good
form; they are material prerequisites for getting the truth across
a microphone.[4] The sounds come over the air without being

[3] This is all the more astonishing because the Sunday Mass Program
(10:00 to 11:00 A.M.) has a relatively large regular audience. In the
winter of 1963, 14% of the total population between 14 and 70 years
of age listened to the liturgy broadcast (with sermon) in North and
West Germany. In the winter of 1966, 6% still tuned in. The majority
of this audience is composed of women and inhabitants of towns and
rural communities. A considerable audience of older people, retired or
living in old age homes, raises the mean age of those listening to this
liturgical broadcast. Paralleling this drop in the radio audience is the
percentage drop in attendance of Sunday Mass in the large cities. Worth
noting is the reason given by many for listening to this broadcast:
they want to hear a good sermon. The parallel drop in the general radio
audience is matched and conditioned to a large extent by the growing
audience figures for television.

[4] Cf. Hans Jürgen Schultz, "Die unbewältigte Öffentlichkeit der Kirche:
Der Rundfunk als Beispiel," in *Jenseits des Weihrauchs* I edited by Ingo
Hermann and Heinz Robert Schlette (Olten and Freiburg, 1966), pp.
17ff; *ibid.*, p. 7.

fleshed out; their tone and content have no connection with the real world of the listener. Yet, at the same time, they enjoy the advantage of having anonymous authority, and for this reason the microphone has often been misused by those who would seek to win over men.

A Message Taken Relatively

The contents of radio broadcasts do not harmonize with one another. They must compete with each other, for the listener cannot take in everything that is broadcast, and the messages are sometimes contradictory. Bias also affects the listener. He relates what he hears to a total picture. A religious broadcast does not reach its audience in the peculiar precincts of a sacral atmosphere; consciously or unconsciously, the audience measures it against the real world in which it finds expression. By the very nature of the microphone, the message is taken relatively, and this fact is not altered because one claims to be speaking about absolutes. Not only is the broadcaster's word enmeshed in the discontinuity and fluidity of a pluralistic world; the content of his message is also relativized and related to a total picture.

The public nature of a broadcast also rules out the possibility of conformity and unanimity. These things can only be verified when the speaker selects his audience beforehand and thereby excludes those of a different opinion.

A Society in Search of Information

Broadcast preaching requires the toning down of many features that have been part of traditional preaching practice. Modern society is trying to inform itself about many things, and the broadcast media cannot be matched for intensity and effectiveness. If the Church wants to take part in society's quest for information, it must accept the conditions imposed by the broadcast microphone. It is no small thing to ask, but the freedom provided by a pluralistic society offers the Church a unique

opportunity to learn more about herself. Up to now this opportunity has not been fully appreciated or rightly used.

When discussions about religious programming are held,
Church representatives seem to be driven by the Church's right
to "present her case"; in practice, this often turns out to be pure
self-assertion, unrelated to the Church's message and to the conditions imposed by the broadcast microphone. The microphone
requires new approaches in addressing an audience, and the key
concept is *information*.[5]

The desire for information is part of the quest for knowledge,
clarification and maturity. Information makes knowledge possible, allows people to make personal decisions, and helps them to
freely decide their destiny instead of being led by others.

III

REFLECTIONS FOR THE PULPIT PREACHER

Dialogue versus Monologue

The broadcast environment is a new one for the preacher.
Speaking before a microphone is not the same as speaking before
a congregation, but it is not entirely different either. Broadcast
preaching points up clearly the general problems associated with
oral exposition. It lends new intensity to the question of how
relevant present-day preaching is, and it also underlines the
difficulties involved in preaching today.

The congregation continues to lose the social cohesiveness it
once had; the web of structured relationships is disappearing.
In the liturgical assembly we do not encounter a structured, integrated community; instead we encounter individuals or small
groups gathered together for a liturgical service. The congregation has become more public, the individual more private.

Even pulpit preaching now calls for objectivity and dispassion-
ate distance. Devotional talks and fire-and-brimstone sermons

---

[5] On the concept of information as used here, cf. Hans Jürgen
Schultz, *op. cit.*

are out of place, as many preachers readily admit. Even the content of pulpit talks is being taken relatively more and more, and the listener is judging it in terms of his own life and experience.

Addressing a congregation is talking directly to an audience that is present before you; speaking into a microphone is talking indirectly to an audience that is not present before you. Both, however, are monologue situations, because talking is not necessarily intercommunication or dialogue.

Both pulpit preaching and broadcast preaching, however, should be dialogue situations. If they are not, then they are taking place in a vacuum. If a monologue is to provide intercommunication, it must be preceded by an interior dialogue in which the thoughts and feelings of the audience, their freedom and their possible objections, are taken seriously and given room. Rhetorical devices and mass appeals do not create a dialogue; in fact, they often lead to duplicity. They try to captivate instead of convincing, to exert persuasiveness instead of stimulating free consent, to win custody of the listener instead of helping him to make a mature decision.

The Role of Theology

Free, conscious consent and mature decision-making presuppose that the person has acquired the necessary information first. A broad fund of information is a necessity for life in modern society. Both the sophisticated and the unsophisticated listener need information, and they have been grooved in this direction. The many shapes which information takes call for some sort of context, some sort of integration into a whole. Multiplicity itself does not create a world; there must be some sense of proportion between the individual entities. By the very nature of her mission, the Church is obliged to provide some integrating context for the plurality to be found in modern-day life.

Over against modern man's conquest of the world, we find the Church withdrawing from the world. While modern man engages in a process of self-discovery, the Church stands off to the side. As an institution, she is not involved in this process; as a source of knowledge and information, she is involved only slightly. The work of many individual theologians (scholars for the most part) is not regarded as the Church's contribution to man's quest for emancipation and self-realization. While these theologians are respected and befriended by other scholars, the Church herself is regarded with mistrust and disillusionment. Many do not articulate this feeling because they no longer entertain the idea that the Church will provide an integrating context for their life and the ambivalence of their varied experiences.

As a social institution the Church has found a place for herself in many spheres and many localities, and she has exerted some initiative in this respect. But in modern society's quest for information and for the meaning of life, the Church has remained in the splendid isolation of her age-old claims. Many people feel that she is trying to give more than she has, that she has forgotten that truth also has its proper proportions.

There are lessons here for pulpit preaching and broadcast preaching. Instead of providing answers for obscure puzzles, we must look for the hidden answer to the one real puzzle. Instead of presenting our case with arguments from the past, we must look for theological information that will provide a context for life. People are not looking for edifying words; they are looking for answers. If one is addressing people who have acquired varied and differing stores of information, he must approach them with modesty and with a personal store of information. Today preaching is not so much exhortation as it is an objective communication and a personal witness that must hold its own over against the store of information possessed by others.

Therefore, there are no formulas and no models. As one broadcast editor said when he was asked how a priest should speak on the air: "His talk should involve me; it should involve you; it should involve the times in which we are living." Even today we are still captivated by the erroneous notion that all we need do is dress up the old message in modern clothes, that this will bring it up to date. But this sort of updating only highlights the outdated nature of what is being said.

Preaching can be no better than the theology which lies behind it. Indeed, it is often worse than the underlying theology, sharing nothing but a few terms and concepts. But theology is not its sole support. It is conditioned even more by the surrounding milieu and by the real or imagined outlook and expectations of the audience. These things are not readily subject to rational analysis and control, and when the speaker approaches the broadcast microphone, where he is isolated from these things, the dilemma becomes quite apparent.

Concerned about the milieu and the supposed expectations of his audience, the radio preacher (even the young preacher who is fresh from his theology courses) adopts terms and vocabulary that are pseudo-psychological and pseudo-spiritual. The frequent infelicities in his speech seem to indicate both personal and theological insecurity. It seems he cannot avoid the temptation to mix dogmatic statements with experiential comments in helter-skelter fashion, and to fall back on broad generalities.

The Emphasis on Personal Salvation

Present-day preaching also poses questions about form and method. But even more important is the theological concern as to whether we can express what we want to say. The mutual relationship between the content of preaching and the way it is expressed is not a casual one by any means. The problem of theology is not restricted to *what* is preached. It also involves another question that has not yet been given due consideration: *How* are we to approach the whole matter theologically in order to arrive at information that is suitable and communicable to our audience?

In present-day preaching the evils of the day and the wickedness of man are painted in richer colors than ever before, and the message of salvation and peace is put in the background. This approach reflects an evaluation of the people to whom we are speaking. Justification and redemption are watered down, becoming a reward for those who stay aloof from the evils of the day and the wickedness of other men. Christianity thus becomes a very private affair, despite occasional references to the Christian's responsibility for the world and society through his own apostolate. Yet it is a world which was largely a product of the Church until recent years, a world in which Christians have some say but tend to associate salvation with the future rather than with the present.

It is not made clear that Christian life is possible and relevant only in society. People find it easier to discuss the necessity of faith in terms of personal life.[6]

The Church as Fortress

Retaining the old methods that are "tried and true", many preachers react to the waning interest of society in the Church by calling for conversion. They stand on the pinnacle of the temple and call to those outside; however, they do not leave its guarded precincts, nor do they attempt to formulate the message of salvation and peace in a way that is relevant for a society in the process of emancipating itself. It is not surprising that broadcast editors regard such sermons and talks as the weakest link in their programming chain.

When the Church is identified with a social order that has long since passed, she is hemmed in behind the borderlines of that order. Those norms she advocates that possess social usefulness are recognized even beyond those borderlines; they are regarded as self-evident, humanist postulates. Insofar as the Church has limited her preaching to the realm of individual salvation, she is regarded as a training ground that performs a pedagogical service for society.

[6] A tabulation of concepts and terms that cropped up in a morning religious program showed these results. Most frequently used were words and themes such as suffering, death, sickness, loneliness, misfortune, doubt, despair and daily toil. They cropped up even more frequently in Protestant programs than in Catholic ones.

A World of Searchers

Present-day aloofness from the Church is not to be explained in terms of man's callousness and hardness of heart. What are questionable are the Church's attitude and relationship to the world, her lack of interest in it, and the form and content of her message.

It is simply wrong to blame the lack of interest in the Church on present-day standards and living conditions. The fact is that there is an astonishing revival of interest in theological questions. Church pronouncements get a very favorable reception when they have something to say about questions that are relevant for men today. Theological books that are not devotional or esoteric, that do not restrict themselves to ghetto talk, find a ready market.

While there is relatively little audience response to liturgical or sermon broadcasts, many listeners will write for a copy of some informational broadcast on theology. They want to reread the discussion in the peace and quiet of their own home.

Ghetto Talk

Present-day preaching, on the air and in the pulpit, uses a distinctive language to a large extent. Its users say that it suits the content of their message. In reality, it strikes no response in its listeners. It is a prefabricated language to a large extent, an esoteric language of specialists that gives no information to those who do not know the discipline.

The terms are code words whose meaning is not questioned because they are familiar code words. Those who have not grown up in the Church regard her conceptual framework as empty talk that cannot be verified in reality. Insofar as preaching has adopted its own special word code that is not the code of real scientific theology, it is spouting ghetto talk that has no impact on the world outside the ghetto. Its abstruseness proves that it is out of this world. Using it, a preacher can talk a lot and not say a single thing. It is idle chatter.

IV

SUMMARY

The listener must be a partner in the preaching process. Preaching must be speech, and speech is a process of informing and communicating. It seeks to provide information and understanding, and this presupposes intelligibility.

Preaching is not meant to demonstrate the faith; it is a way of bearing witness to the faith. We can lay down this general principle: What is to be believed must be expressible in words —or, to put it another way: If a person cannot say what he believes, then what he says will not be believed.

The Gospel is a message to mankind, not a possession of the Church. The peculiar terminology of preaching is regarded as the speech of faith; in reality, it only proves the present-day muteness of faith, for it does not articulate the faith in words. We cannot compensate for this muteness by talking more and more about the faith; our constant talk is a substitute for communication. But the Gospel is a message communicated to the world, not the privileged possession of some ghetto.

When the broadcast microphone is used for preaching, it points up our present inability to express the faith in words. We must put the faith into words, not make up words about the faith.

PART II
BIBLIOGRAPHICAL
SURVEY

Karl Rahner, S.J./*Münster, W. Germany*
Karl Lehmann/*Munich, W. Germany*

Preaching and Preaching Aids: Introductory Remarks

This Bibliographical Survey attempts to supplement the more systematic essays in this volume by examining the more important institutions, conferences and periodicals which have tried to improve the preaching situation in various countries since World War II. Well-qualified observers will report critically on the situation in a linguistic region or large country. This task has been interpreted differently by the various authors. While some confined themselves to a more or less complete factual survey, others tried to go more deeply into the concrete circumstances, the background and the results of the various attempts at renewal. The keynote is also different; critical considerations stand side by side with somewhat enthusiastic reports, and comprehensive programs accompany rather meager inventories. In spite of great efforts there are whole continents for which we lack adequate information. Thus, apart from Brazil and Chile (particularly the archdiocese of Santiago) there is little information about Latin America; many countries did not reply at all to our inquiries. These large blank patches on the map demand a cautious interpretation of what facts we have. Some unfortunate overlapping through defective organization led to a failure to mention some situations, as in the case of Belgium. All in all, we might summarize the more striking evidence as follows:

1. While in the field of catechetics and liturgy there have been serious attempts at renewal for some time, the institutional aids for preaching in any comprehensive sense have hardly been tackled, and then mainly as a kind of appendix to some catechetical or liturgical reform. All attempts at renewal of preaching in the strict sense are still only in the opening phase.

2. In general, the various attempts made clearly underrate the importance of a simultaneous deepening of theology. This leads to the danger that a given theological situation is simply preserved and repeated as the norm for preaching. New developments in linguistic philosophy and in the biblical and systematic theology of the Word of God, with their pastoral consequences, are clearly only applied peripherally.

3. Those attempts at renewal that we know of rightly concentrate on preaching in the form of the homily, while other subjects for sermons, taken from the wider teaching of faith, moral theology, the sacraments, and so on, occupy a curiously modest place; in fact, they are hardly mentioned.

4. It is probably a result of the formerly prevailing notion of formal and practical homiletics that aids for preaching are so often only seen as a matter of more practical and "technical" instructions. This leads to a great deal of time spent on schemes or even ready-made recipes. There is too little concentration on a more intense and basic theological effort, united with prayer, meditation and pastoral experience (see n. 2 above).

5. It appears that in other fields, too, there is still a tight clinging to the old image of the sermon. The new data provided by the psychology and sociology of the mass-media, information and publicity are rarely applied, with the result that the preacher remains for a large part ignorant of the real situation of those who listen to him, the way they understand his explanation, and the relation between what he says and the laws that operate in the mind of his audience.

Such a survey is bound to remain general and will not do justice to every attempt at renewal. Nevertheless, the overall picture clearly shows that all theological disciplines must come to the rescue of our preaching if it wants to be better equipped to transmit the Christian message in this age.

Luis Maldonado/*Madrid, Spain*

Preaching in Spain

I t is curious to note that there exist no centers or institutions with
the specific and exclusive purpose
of forming preachers. They do, of course, exist for catechetics.
And it is an encouraging sign that some of these latter are tending to turn into centers of pastoral mission theology, the title
clearly indicating that what they are interested in and working
for is not just the doctrinal teaching of the catechism (to a
limited age-group) but the whole pastoral theology of the Word
in all its manysidedness.

Within this line of development stands the Institutio Superior
de Pastoral, specifically its catechetics department. A dependency
of the Pontifical University of Salamanca, it is located in Madrid.
It works as a center of pastoral specialization, following up the
courses of the theological faculty. The department's basic courses
are in biblical theology, anthropology, the theology of mission,
an introduction to the liturgy, an introduction to the lay apostolate, the theology of terrestrial realities, pastoral catechetical
theology (nature and history of catechesis), Christian initiation,
teaching theory (both general and for specific age groups) and
communications media.

The bishops' education commission organizes annually through
the National Catechetical Secretariat three summer courses in
different areas of the peninsula with a body of specialized teach-

ers. Both priests and laity take part in them. They study fundamental problems of pastoral mission and others more narrowly catechetical.

Acting in close connection with this work are the St. Pius X Pontifical Institute of Tejares (Salamanca), run by the Brothers of the Christian Schools and the theological faculty of Vitoria, the latter placing more emphasis in its summer courses on biblical initiation and biblical teaching methods.

The religious a short while ago requested a national congress to deal with the problem of parochial and internal missions. Thanks to a young team of Redemptorists, by and large the life and soul of the Congress, one can see an unmistakable renewal in this type of missionary preaching.

In the dioceses, one feature of current curial reorganization is the tendency to nominate an episcopal vicar or delegate for pastoral missionary activity.

On the diocesan level one quite frequently comes across crash courses, lasting about a week, to bring home to priests the new understanding and the new theology of the Word, its sacramental character, its kerygmatic structure, its relationship with biblical methods of instruction, etc.

With regard to the Sunday homily, the technique of group preparation and group postmortem seems to be spreading. These groups can also have lay members. Normally three points are discussed: the exegesis of the given pericope, its connection with concrete problems of daily life and its connection with the liturgy.

In some communities there is a growing custom to have laymen say a few words after the priest's sermon, bringing their own living experience to bear on what they have just heard. This is becoming possible thanks to the division of parishes and the multiplication of Mass centers.

Obligatory sermon plans for the year's preaching, such as used to appear in diocesan bulletins, have practically disappeared. Their ineffectiveness and collapse have been total.

Notwithstanding all the positive elements listed so far, it can still be said that preaching is in a state of crisis and that priests are thoroughly confused by the situation at the same time as feeling without resources or qualifications to deal with it. What they are offered by official sources to deal with the problem is in general quite insufficient, not to say useless. One can now see just how little preaching counted for in a pastoral outlook whose whole approach was sacramentalist.

The main theoretical works on preaching, published in central Europe, have appeared in translation. As for works written during recent years in Spain, the present writer deeply regrets that he only knows one of his own: *El Mensaje de los Cristianos. Introducción a la Pastoral de la Predicación* (Barcelona, 1965).

As tools for the preparation of the Sunday sermon there are the eleven little volumes of Fr. T. Cabestrero's excellent book, *Palabra de Vida* (Madrid, 1966–67); it further takes into account the *lectio continua* recently introduced.

Two great collections are in process of translation: *Las Asambleas del Señor* (Madrid, 1965ff.) and *Palabra de Dios* (Salamanca, 1966ff.) (from the German work, *Am Tisch des Wortes*). All five volumes of the work of Th. Maertens–J. Frisque, *Guía de la asamblea cristiana* (Bilbao-Madrid, 1964–67) have been published in translation and are having a great influence.

Among reviews, one should single out *Pentecostés, Sinite, Pastoral Misionera, Iglesia Viva* and *Phase*. A collection whose quality and up-to-dateness make it a positive influence is that of *Cuadernos de Teología y Práctica pastoral,* published in Madrid.

The P.P.C. publishing house in Madrid has brought out four volumes entitled *Catequesis y Formación Conciliar* (Madrid, 1966) and intends to get into preaching circulation the main ideas of Vatican Council II. The authors are C. Godoy, J. M. Setien and M. Useros.

Domenico Grasso, S.J. / *Rome, Italy*

Preaching in Italy

The term "preaching" is used to indicate the proclamation of the Gospel to the Christian community, and thus differs from *evangelization* which is intended for pagans, and from *catechesis* which is directed to catechumens or to those of the baptized who have not yet ratified their baptism. The people commonly refer to it as "the sermon". This forms the subject of the present article.

In Italy there are no special institutes to prepare the clergy for preaching as there are for catechesis. Such preparation generally takes place in seminaries, in the study of "pastoral theology" which is taught for a period of four years. One year is completely devoted to the subject of preaching to the Christian community, in which the Sunday homily occupies a prominent position. This instruction is often the responsibility of a priest who is entrusted with the care of souls.

In seminaries which have not yet updated their instruction in the art of preaching, homiletics is limited to the formal aspect. Stress is placed on the *manner* of preaching and on the problems of style and diction. Frequently, courses in diction are given by specialists who teach in schools that prepare personnel for radio and the stage.[1] Rarely in this teaching are problems of

---

[1] It is interesting to note that one of the best books on sacred oratory in Italy was written by a well-known actor (C. Tamberlani, *L'oratore sacro,* Rome, 1964).

content treated, for the professor takes for granted that they are already known. However, even before the Council a need was felt for a treatment which would extend to these problems as well. This stemmed in large part from the rise of the kerygmatic movement in Italy, which has had repercussions even on preaching.

Homiletics has enjoyed special development wherever—in accord with the dispositions of the *Sedes Sapientiae*—the so-called "fifth year" for the immediate preparation of young priests for the apostolate has been instituted, and in the pastoral institutes which are springing up everywhere in the various regions of Italy. In the Lateran Institute, which was the first to emerge, homiletics is treated in the course entitled "de sacra eloquentia", in that of "fundamental pastoral theology", and in the special course on the "theology of preaching". These courses are also found—although possibly even more synthetically—in the other pastoral institutes.

Besides being treated in general reviews of theology and religious culture,[2] as well as those on preaching that are directed to the clergy,[3] problems of preaching are also discussed in periodicals exclusively devoted to the ministry of the Word. We might mention the monthly *Ministerium Verbi* and the bimonthly *Temi di predicazione*. The former was founded forty-one years ago and is an offshoot of the review *Palestra del clero* which is published at Rovigo. Its purpose is to provide priests who have the care of souls with schemas for preaching that can inspire their preaching in the customary Sunday homily and in the various feasts of the liturgical year.

Much more important is *Temi di predicazione* published by the Dominicans of Naples in monographic issues. Established in 1956, the review is the work of outstanding theologians and scholars and proposes to present the various themes of Christian preaching, both dogmatic and moral, in their biblical and patris-

[2] Among others, we might mention *La Civiltà Cattolica, La Scuola Cattolica, Il Regno* and *Humanitas*.

[3] Outstanding in this regard are *Palestra del clero, Settimana del clero, Pietà sacerdotale* and *Rivista di pastorale liturgica*.

tic sources as well as in the *Acta* of the magisterium of the Church; its purpose is to aid preachers to perceive their real content and the significance they hold in Catholic teaching and in the Christian life. A mere glance at the index of the various issues will demonstrate the enormous variety of themes treated up to the present: God, the Church, the eucharist, grace, the family, the last things, the theological virtues, the Sacred Heart, the sacraments, the commandments, the religious life, dialogue. The final issue of each year is devoted to theological problems of preaching. It is the most important issue and the one which gives the periodical a thoroughly theological aspect. Thus far nine such issues have been published, and they contain genuine contributions for a theology of preaching.

We might mention in particular the commentary on the documents of Vatican Council II published by this periodical, which constitutes a precious source for all who desire to make the conciliar teaching the object of their preaching to the people. The same Dominicans of *Temi di predicazione* are also responsible for an edition of the documents of the Council which has enjoyed wide success. They are presently preparing a third edition with the addition of a whole series of postconciliar documents.

Together with reviews, preaching in Italy can make use of conferences which year by year continue to multiply in the various dioceses and ecclesiastical regions. Italy does not yet have a homiletic association which holds regular conventions; however, it does possess pastoral centers which often make preaching the theme of their conventions.

The first of these is the *Centro di Orientamento pastorale* (COP), founded at Milan by Monsignor Grazioso Ceriani, which runs an annual convention on a national level dealing with pastoral problems in Italy and is attended by hundreds of priests. The Center treated the preaching theme for the first time during the 1956 Congress. In it bishops, theologians, and pastors —all highly qualified—dealt with the proclamation of the Word of God both in the ordinary preaching to the parish community and in preaching to various groups. Among the latter we might mention the reports and relative discussions concerning preaching to young people, workers, country folk, intellectuals and students. The Proceedings of that convention constitute a source of inspiration that even now, years later, retains its up-to-date character. The same Center also dealt with preaching in last year's convention.

Another Center that warrants mention is the *Regalità di Cristo,* whose secretary is the Franciscan R. Falsini. It holds a yearly convention, which is very well attended by priests, to discuss questions of pastoral liturgy. This year the theme of the convention was the Sunday homily.

Even the review *Temi di predicazione* has in its program the organization of conventions on preaching. Up to the present it has held two, at Salerno and Florence, on the question of how to combat atheistic Communism, which is a very real problem in Italy.

The same work of *aggiornamento* which these Centers carry on for the diocesan clergy is carried forward by the Secretariats of the various religious orders and congregations who seek to adjust their preaching to the changed conditions of the Christian life of our time. The Franciscan Friars Minor had a Secretariat for preaching over a period of twenty years; after various vicissitudes, this was transformed into an Institute of a theological character with its seat at the *Antonianum* in Rome. A few years ago this Institute held a Congress on the updating of preaching for all the Friars Minor in Italy. An identical Secretariat has recently been established by the Capuchin Friars.

This same work of study and updating of their preaching is being carried on by other religious orders and congregations. Some years ago, conventions on the renewal of the popular missions were held by the Missionaries of the Precious Blood and by the Priests of the Mission (Lazarists). We have learned that the Redemptorists and Passionists have done the same.

For the present, it is difficult to estimate the effects of this fermentation of renewal taking place in the area of preaching in Italy. Undoubtedly, much work remains to be done before results can really be seen. However, the interest shown by the general public toward preaching[4] and the steadily increasing publications on the subject[5] are indications that the problem is known and that the desired renewal will not be long in coming to pass.

[4] We refer to two studies on preaching conducted by *L'Osservatore Romano della domenica* (February 5, 1967) and by the very popular weekly *Famiglia cristiana* (April 19, 1967).

[5] A few of the more recent monographs are: Sandro Maggiolini, *La predicazione nella vita della Chiesa* (Brescia, 1961); Raimondo Spiazzi, *Verbum salutis* (Rome, 1963); Domenico Grasso, *L'Annuncio della salvezza* (Naples, 1965)—English edition: *Proclaiming God's Message —A Study in the Theology of Preaching* (Notre Dame, 1965).

François Coudreau / *Boulogne-sur-Seine, France*

Preaching in France

The renewal of preaching in the Church in France has taken place over the course of two periods:

1. During the period after World War I, between 1945 and 1960, in the light of the *catechetical* renewal. The profound and dynamic reflection on the content and presentation of catechesis, in the most exacting twofold respect of the object of faith (revelation) and the act of faith (conversion), has had an enormous effect on preaching. Sermon books were gradually abandoned, and the preacher sought the way of the message that enlightens, challenges, invites, and leads.

2. During the conciliar and postconciliar period, since 1961, in the light of the *liturgical* renewal. The profound and dynamic reflection on the paschal mystery and the act of celebration has reintroduced preaching into the mystery celebrated; thus nowadays we are slowly rediscovering the homily—real encounter between the Word of God heard, discovered and contemplated —and the concrete life-event in which man is inserted to build the kingdom therein.

These are two sources of renewal, but one spirit animates both —the spirit of an *actualization of the Word of God* for the *"consecratio mundi"*. On the following pages we will discuss the instruments and the spirit of this renewal.

I

THE INSTRUMENT OF THE PREACHING RENEWAL

Let us first provide a simple listing of names in the reverse order of importance and efficacy: (1) Books; (2) Periodicals; (3) Centers; (4) Institutes; (5) Schemas; (6) Sessions; (7) The Holy Father.

1. *Books*

These were numerous and must therefore be classified under two categories:

(a) Books *on* preaching, as, for example:

Gritti (Jules): *Prêcher aux hommes de notre temps,* Ed. Privat, 1960, 159 pp. (questions posed to Catholics).

Semmelroth (Otto), S.J.: *Parole efficace: pour une théologie de la prédication,* Ed. St. Paul, 1962, 247 pp., translated from the German.

(b) Books *for* preaching, as, for example:

Girard (Raymond), P.S.S.: *Prêcher Jésus,* Ed. Fleurus, 1965, 206 pp.

2. *Periodicals*

(a) Many French periodicals deal with preaching problems, directly or indirectly:

Catéchèse: 19 rue de Varenne, Paris, 7ème.

Maison-Dieu: 11 rue Perronnet, Neuilly, 92.

L'Union: 31 rue de Fleurus, Paris, 6ème.

Paroisse et Mission, 4 rue des Prêtres St. Severin, Paris, 5ème.

Parole et Mission, 29 bd. de la Tour Maubourg, Paris, 7ème.

Prêtres diocésains, 179 rue de Tolbiec, Paris, 13ème.

Prêtres aujourd'hui, 21 rue du Faubourg St. Antoine, Paris, 11ème.

(b) But foreign periodicals, in French, are read and exert profound influence in France:

Lumen Vitae, 184 rue Washington, Brussels I, Belgium. (We will merely mention one article among many: Fournier (Elie), *"Quand le Concile parle de l'homélie,"* in Lumen Vitae, No. 4, 1963, pp. 739–755.)

Paroisse et Liturgie: Abbaye de Saint André, Bruges 3, Belgium.

Biblica: Abbaye de Saint André, Bruges 3, Belgium.

3. Centers

Three centers publish and edit documents and outlines for preaching and catechesis:

Le C.N.E.R.: Centre d'Enseignement Religieux, Paris, 7ème, 19 rue de Varenne;

Le C.N.P.L.: Centre national de Pastorale Liturgique, 11 rue Perronnet, Neuilly, 92;

Le Service National du Catéchuménat, 37 rue Linné, Paris, 5ème.

In addition, the Centre Lumen Vitae, and the Cahiers de la Rosarie, in Belgium, 184 rue Washington, render the same service.

4. Institutes

Institutes of catechesis in the four Catholic universities and the University of Strasbourg provide a wide variety of possibilities for priests who wish to benefit from a "reorientation" and thus renew their preaching:

Paris: Institut Supérieur de Pastorale catéchétique, 26 rue d'Assas, 6ème.

Lille: Licence d'Enseignement religieux, 60 bd. Vauban.

Ecole des Missionaires d'Action catholique et d'Action sociale (EMACAS), 28 bis rue Emile Zola, 59, Mons en Bareuil.

Angers: Cours de Catéchèse de la Faculté de Théologie de l'Université catholique, 6 rue Volney.

Lyon: Licence d'Enseignement Religieux des Facultés catholiques, 25 rue du Plot.

Strasbourg: Institut de Pastorale catéchétique, 11 bd. du Président Edwards.

5. *Schemas*

Special mention must be made of the attempts to provide schemas for preaching which are very successful in France:

(a) The periodical *L'Union,* 31 rue de Fleurus, Paris, 6ème, offers a bimonthly rubric on the "Sunday Homily".

(b) Two recent series are: *En Eglise chaque dimanche* (1966) and *Prêcher Jésus* (1967).

(c) *Le Service de l'Homélitique* (1 rue Stewart, Ottawa, Canada) offers very elaborate monthly plans for preaching.

6. *Sessions*

The most *concrete* and *effective* work toward the renewal of preaching undoubtedly takes place in the multiple diocesan and interdiocesan sessions, initiated by bishops, under the direction of specialists and working committees of the national centers of catechesis, liturgy, the catechumenate, and the Bible. We find echoes of these sessions:

(a) in the *Semaines Religieuses* (S.R.); for example:

Metz: Ruer (Canon E.), *L'Homélie: une forme de dialogue* (S.R. de Metz, 1–10–64, pp. 4–7);

Paris: Holstein (R; P. Henri), *L'Homélie: réflexions proposées au cours d'une réunion de doyenné de Drancy* (S.R. de Paris, 5/21/64);

Rouen: "Pourquoi passer du sermon à l'Homélie? Pour les lectures et l'Homélie, un pupitre, pourquoi?" (Fiches de la S.R. de Rouen, 12/29/64 and 6/12/65);

Paris: "Dialogues sur la prédication: compte-rendu des ré-

ponses à un questionnaire d'enquête des laïcs et du clergé
(S.R. de Paris, 3/20/65, 12/18/65, 1/1/66);

(b) in *Notes de Pastorale Liturgique*: for example, No. 62,
June, 1966, pp. 12–14: "Préparation de l'Homélie en commun":
testimony of a group of priests from Bayonne who meet to prepare a homily.

7. *The Holy Father*

Pope Paul VI himself often returns to the preaching theme.
The periodical *La Documentation catholique* (D.C.)—5 rue
Bayard, Paris, 8ème—provides precious echoes of this teaching.
We will mention merely the following:

Paul VI: "Importance de la prédication dans 'Ecclesiam
suam' " (D.C. No. 1431, 8/6/64, col. 1085);

Paul VI: "Le Ministère de la Parole: allocution aux curés et
prédicateurs de carême de Rome le 12/2/64" (D.C. No.
1419, 3/1/64, col. 289–292);

Paul VI: "Allocution aux curés et prédicateurs de carême de
Rome le 1/3/65" (D.C., No. 1444, 3/21/65, col. 523–
528).

II

THE SPIRIT OF THE PREACHING RENEWAL

This is the most important aspect of preaching in France, and
it is not the province of this article to define it. Nevertheless, to
present a true picture of what exists in France concerning
preaching, we must mention at this point the primary bases and
fundamental characteristics of this renewal.

It is first and foremost an idea-force of priests who renew
their preaching; this cannot be done without a deep grasp of
the *liturgical action* and the paschal celebration in which it is
inspired.

Second, the attentive reading of *the event* in order to confront it with the Word of God constitutes a condition for the renewal of preaching.

Finally, only a *collaborative effort* on the part of priests and laity involving research, preparation, control and criticism can yield that constant creation of preaching to which the living Word of God invites us.

This effort has begun at its base, and it is this slow and patient effort which constitutes the dominant trait of what is being done in France in the interests of preaching.

Michael Frickel, O.S.B./*Münsterschwarzach, W. Germany*

Updating Preaching Courses in the German-Speaking World

According to Vatican Council II, "it is the first task of priests . . . to preach the Gospel of God to all men" (*Decree on the Ministry and Life of Priests,* n. 4). Preparing priests for this task, then, must be the primary objective of pre- and post-ordination training. This fact has not yet been fully realized, much less carried out in practice. Homiletic training simply must be updated, and competition from the mass media lends a note of urgency to the task.

All this is not an entirely new idea. Even before Vatican Council II, earnest initiatives in this area were undertaken in West Germany. In 1955 and 1956 conventions on preaching were held at Castle Rothenfels, and they were well attended. In 1956, for the first time, there was a meeting of priests who taught preaching. It soon became evident that none of these teachers had the proper formal training for this assignment. Their teaching was a sideline, or just one more duty among many.

This sorry state of affairs was verified once again when the first meeting of German homiletic professors took place in January 1957. The meeting was held in Würzburg, and 30 professors participated. In its final position paper, entitled "Sermon Training Today", the group examined many details of principle and practice, and then formulated these basic postulates:

1. We eventually must work out a theology of God's Word, and this must include a theology of preaching.

2. A comprehensive homiletics program cannot be taught as a sideline, or without thorough preparation and training.

3. Preparing for the preaching office is a full-time project. However, it is never too early to begin learning and using the rudiments of preaching—rhetoric, extempore speech, etc.

Out of this meeting came the "Workshop of Catholic Homiletic Teachers In Germany" (AKHD—"Arbeitsgemeinschaft Katholischer Homiletiker Deutschlands"), with headquarters at 18 Domerschulstrasse, Würzburg. Communication between the members was kept up through a newsletter and a series of book notices on the field of homiletics. However, the real driving force and forum of intercommunication have been the six conventions held under AKHD auspices. Each convention has tackled a specific theme; papers are presented by experts, and a thorough discussion follows. So far the following topics have been examined: Preaching and Theology (1958); Preaching and the Audience (1960); Preaching and Speech (1962); Preaching and Meditation (1964); Preaching and the Mass (1966); Homiletics: Fundamentals and Aims (1967).

The proceedings of the first three meetings have already appeared in print. At the 1967 meeting it was decided that an annual journal would be undertaken; entitled *Verkünden,* it is being published by Verlag Katholisches Bibelwerk of Stuttgart.

At the 1966 meeting, AKHD was expanded to include the whole German-speaking world. Ten years of collaboration and joint effort had gone under the bridge; the basic aims were shared by others in the German-speaking world, even though Austria and Switzerland did not have similar associations. The goals of the organization were set forth in its bylaws:

1. To discuss theoretical and practical questions connected with homiletics, and to promote scientific study of them.

2. To further homiletic training at every level.

3. To encourage and sponsor pertinent publications.

4. To coordinate any and all initiatives taken with respect to present-day preaching.

Membership remains open to all, and would seem to be especially desirable for anyone engaged in homiletic teaching. Others can also become members of the organization.

In the same year a homiletic division was added to the "German Catechetical Institute". This was done with the approval and support of the German Episcopal Conference, and the organization became the "Institute for Catechetics and Homiletics" (IKH). A long-time effort on the part of AKHD had finally borne fruit. At IKH, one can now take a special two-year course on the theory and practice of homiletics, including a final qualifying examination. Anyone assigned to teach homiletics in the future should be equipped with this specialized training. Later on, in addition to its scientific studies, the Institute is to plan and conduct sermon courses. Small-scale efforts in this direction are already under way.

In the German-speaking world, various pastoral conferences have been held on a regular or occasional basis. Among these, the Vienna Conference, held each year around Christmas, has come to have special significance. In 1966 it devoted its attention to the theme of "God's Word in Our Day".[1]

Most periodicals on preaching are of the old-fashioned type, presenting fully worked-out sermons or sermon outlines.[2] *Dienst am Wort*, founded by B. Dreher, adopts a different approach.[3] Here greater personal effort is called for. In each issue five Scripture texts are examined exegetically, a meditation seeks to relate the content of the texts to the present-day situation, and suggestive outlines for actual sermons are presented; a scholarly article on homiletics closes out the issue. Reviews of pertinent books are now also included.

[1] Cf. Christmas Pastoral Conference in Vienna, "Gottes Wort in unserer Zeit," in *Herder-Korr.* 21 (1967), pp. 108–11; the Proceedings of the Conference are available from Seelsorgerverlag Herder, Vienna.

[2] Deserving of special mention is the Scripture series, *Biblische Predigt*, edited by B. Dreher for Seelsorge-Verlag, Freiburg.

[3] A bimonthly biblical-homiletical periodical put out by Seelsorge-Verlag, Freiburg. Yearly subscription, DM 15.

A similar service is provided by the scriptural series *Am Tisch des Wortes*.[4] Six to eight issues appear each year, each one devoted to a particular Sunday or feast day of the Church year. Various articles in each issue examine the feast from a liturgical, scriptural, dogmatic, exegetical and meditational point of view. Sample sermons are appended as an aid to the preacher.

[4] Verlag Katholisches Bibelwerk, Stuttgart.

Herman Borgert, C.SS.R. / *Wittem, Netherlands*

The Sermon in Holland

I t is a curious fact that there is no official body in Holland in charge of the practice of preaching or concerned with the coordination and encouragement of new initiatives in this field. And yet, the difficulties of preaching and the problems connected with it are more noticeable than ever before, and both priests and laity are unhappy about the situation. Until a few years ago there was at least a committee that looked after the preaching of parochial missions —the Committee for Popular Missions—but this group has now been dissolved inasmuch as these popular missions are no longer given in Holland. There have been plans to replace this Committee by another that would be in charge of preaching in all its aspects. But these plans have been left in abeyance since there was no desire to cut across the plans being prepared by the Pastoral Institute of the Dutch Province. In 1965 this Institute set up a commission for preaching whose purpose may be summed up in the following three points: (1) to draw up an inventory of all organized activities in Holland in this field; (2) to find out whether this matter of preaching is given sufficiently serious attention within the whole framework of pastoral care; (3) to investigate the question whether a special "working" commission should be set up to deal with preaching. This investigation led to a positive demand for such a commission,

and one can therefore expect that the Dutch Pastoral Council
which is still in progress will take the necessary measures.

This growing worry about preaching is evidenced by various
incidental activities. In large towns the clergy have been meeting regularly in order to prepare the Sunday sermon collectively.
Every year there are days of study where young priests are
shown how to give retreats. Moreover, various orders and congregations have their own work groups concerned with preaching.

There are two periodicals where priests can find pastoral help
for their preaching: *De Gewijde Rede* (*Sacred Speaking*) and
Kerygma. The former is a monthly review, published by the
Franciscans, which provides plans for sermons, each followed
by an introduction and a worked-out sermon. *Kerygma* contains Sunday sermons based on larger topics—e.g., the world,
the resurrection, peace. These topics are first put into their
theological context and then properly introduced. Waalheuvel,
the military training center, produces *Contact,* which contains
plans for sermons and reflections for army chaplains. In general,
the theory of preaching is indirectly dealt with in articles about
the priestly image of the future. Several theologians think that
this image will in the future show more prophetic features and
therefore that preaching will occupy a more important place
in the training of future priests.

This more scientific training is taking place at the moment
in some five large centers where diocesan and regular training
institutes have been concentrated. This training contains a five-
year basic course and a two-year pastoral course. Particularly
during the first year of this pastoral course, preaching will be
dealt with seriously, not so much in regard to the theoretical
background but rather by training in the various techniques.
The theological faculty of Nijmegen University has a specialized
course in pastoral theology under the direction of Dr. F.
Haarsma. Here, too, preaching in its various forms plays an important part.

New studies appear regularly which deal with the place, function and content of preaching and its relation to theology; many of these studies come from Protestant scholars.

One should mention here the *Peiling naar oordelen over de zondagspreek,* an inquiry on attitudes toward the Sunday sermon, conducted in 1963 and 1964 in Eindhoven, which has a Catholic majority, and in Amsterdam, where the Catholics are in a minority. In March 1964 some six hundred churchgoers were interviewed in Amsterdam on three successive Sundays in six parishes. They were asked to state their reaction to the sermon they had listened to that morning and what they thought about the sermon in general terms. Dr. C. Straver has worked out the data provided by this inquiry in a sociological thesis, *Massacommunicatie en godsdienstige beïnvloeding* (Hilversum/ Antwerp, 1967). Some of the results seem to me important for the preacher. In Eindhover 78.1% and in Amsterdam 77.9% would not want to miss the sermon. But apart from this fact, the figures for the appreciation of the actual sermon heard are far from favorable, and there is much criticism. In general there seems to be a definite wish for sermons with a topical theme connected with life (75%). The predominantly abstract sermon is firmly rejected.

Christian proclamation by radio or television is very important in Holland. At the end of the day the number of listeners and viewers is very high indeed. The above-mentioned inquiry shows that the faithful appreciate "informal preaching" more than the Sunday sermon.

Józef Majka / *Tarnow, Poland*

Preaching in Poland

Polish Canon Law imposes an obligation of preaching every Sunday and feastday both during Mass and on other occasions. This was laid down both by the National Council of 1936[1] and by diocesan synods.[2] These demand the preaching on every Sunday of the year of sermons on the catechism, which are meant to go in cycles of from three to five years. On feastdays they allow a homily on the Gospel of the day. These synodal decrees also contain a general directive that preachers are to make extensive use of Scripture in all sermons.

In order to get good preachers the bishops are setting up in every seminary a chair of homiletics with lectures and practices. The lectures are for the most part based on the manual of Abbé Pilch,[3] though there is another less well-known one by Abbé Rzeszewski.[4]

It is only in the last few years that any university studies and research in this field have been carried out. Before the war, if there were any such in the theological faculties of Polish universities, they were indistinguishable from those of seminaries. The chairs of homiletics recently established at the Catholic Univer-

[1] Cf. *Pierwszy polski synod plenarny* (Lublin, 1939), pp. 109ff.
[2] Cf. *Trzeci synod diecezji tarnowskiej* (Tarnow, 1956), pp. 344–46.
[3] Z. Pilch, *Wyklad zasad wymowy kościelnej* (Poznan, 1958).
[4] M. Rzeszewski, *Kaznodziejstwo, zagadnienia wybrane* (Warsaw, 1957).

sity of Lublin (1960) and at the Academy of Catholic Theology at Warsaw (1966) have a different task. It consists not simply in the preparation of teachers for the big seminaries but also of scientific research in this field. Studies are being prepared here which are intended to cover the whole ground of the theology of preaching and the history of the problem; also under study are the questions connected with adapting methods, means and the whole approach of religious instruction to the needs of the faithful and their social circumstances.[5] It follows that entirely new concepts of preaching are being investigated.

There are annual congresses for professors of homiletics from all the diocesan and religious seminaries; these are dedicated to the same end. They were inaugurated on the occasion of the Polish Theological Congress in 1958. The activity of the professors was powerfully reinforced after the last theological congress in 1966. Its field of study is primarily the theology of preaching and its connection with Scripture, liturgy and the national culture.

Specialized periodicals also have an important part to play in the development of preaching. After the war there were two of this kind: *Ambona Współczesna,* published in Kielce until 1959[6] and *Biblioteka Kaznodziejska* which is still appearing in Poznan.[7] They contain not only sermons of every description but also articles on theory and practice. Articles on preaching appear in other reviews—catechetical, theological and pastoral.[8]

The various dioceses of Poland organized pastoral activities intended to draw the attention of the faithful to particular religious problems. In all these cases the pastoral departments of the diocesan curia would make out a preaching program that

[5] W. Witkowski, *Działalność misyjna ojców redemptorystów w Polsce na tle warunków społeczno-religijnych dwudziestolecia międzywojennego 1918–1939* (Lublin, 1963).

[6] *Ambona Współczesna,* a quarterly review devoted to Polish preaching. It appeared from 1945 to 1959, though suspended from 1951 to 1957.

[7] *Biblioteka Kaznodziejska,* a monthly homiletical review, published at Poznan since 1862.

[8] Cf. *Katecheta,* a fortnightly review devoted to problems of religious instruction; it has appeared since 1957 at Poznan. Also *Ateneum Kapłańskie,* appearing since 1909; *Homo Dei,* an ascetical and pastoral review published by the Redemptorist Fathers at Warsaw.

handed down, right to parish priest level, the ready-made outlines of sermons.

The period of the Great Novena, the preparation for the millennary of the baptism of Poland, had a centrally directed program of pastoral action for the whole country, which included the preaching related to it. Each year of the Great Novena was dedicated to a particular problem; there was the year of grace, of life, of the family, of marriage, of education, of justice, of charity, and so on. These were in principle the themes of all sermons preached during those years. A special commission of the episcopate, assisted by a pastoral commission, was invited to draw up a detailed program of preaching. All these projects were assessed by the two commissions and approved by the bishops. Then the homiletic part was put into the hands of specialists who prepared the necessary materials and the sermon outlines and sometimes even the full text. The materials were published in the homiletic reviews or mimeographed by the diocesan pastoral departments.

These preaching programs made room for "free" Sundays on which the subject of sermons could be fixed by the local bishop or even by the parish priest. Further, each individual diocese tried to adapt its program to the particular needs of its faithful, and this adaptation often went a long way. It also happened that some parish priests, accustomed to the traditional catechetical themes, came to the conclusion that the preaching of the Novena was too difficult and so did their preaching in accordance with their old formularies.

The Novena's program covered not only the basic preaching done at Mass but also instruction for children and youth and even the conferences of retreats. During Lent it is normal in Poland for all parishes to organize retreats for each particular group of the faithful. Retreats and missions are preached for the most part by religious.

A central preaching and pastoral program has been maintained after the end of the Great Novena; it is prepared in the same way by the pastoral commission of the episcopate. There is no doubt that it helps to raise the standard of preaching, to modernize and bring it up to date, to treat its problems at depth and even to improve it stylistically. But it is not without negative features and does present certain dangers. Will not ready-made sermon outlines free preachers from any real preparation of their sermon and even any real thinking on certain basic theological problems? Is there not a risk that this might to a certain extent have given a superficial and overschematic character to all the teaching? Furthermore, there is no escaping the need to adapt preaching to the needs and mentality of one's actual listeners. If a preacher does not tackle the given problem in his own way, there is a possibility that he will make no contact with his audience, that his preaching will not be taken in and understood, that he will not be preaching Christ from his own heart and so will not be Christ's witness.

Those responsible for preparing the sermon programs are well aware of these dangers and try not to give preachers ready-made sermons. They invite them to recast the themes and material received in order to adapt them to their listeners.

The university centers already mentioned and the conferences of professors of homiletics are on the lookout for new forms of preaching and new forms of homily, based on the theological concept of bearing witness to Christ: *"Eritis mihi testes"* (Acts 1, 8). It would still be premature to write anything on the outcome of this research. The work has scarcely begun.

François Lepargneur, O.P./*Montreal, Canada*

Perspectives for the Renewal of Preaching in Brazil

The mediocrity and at times the absence of preaching in assemblies of Catholic worship in Brazil has been known for some time, but it is a first sign of renewal that a growing number of the faithful are taking note of this and aspiring to better things.

Vatican Council II has enabled a good many priests to become concerned about the situation. However, the ferment of the present day allows only an incomplete picture and provisional judgments; there is the risk of being too optimistic in consulting only official texts and too pessimistic in considering merely the results already attained.

The measures of renewal touch preaching only indirectly or in a very wide sense.

1. *Basic catechesis* remains the dominant preoccupation of Brazilian preaching. A Higher Institute of Pastoral Catechetics or its equivalent has been established in Rio de Janeiro, São Paulo, Porto Alegre, Salvador and Belo Horizonte. This service of the Word of God hardly reaches adults or priests since it is generally administered by religious or lay women for the benefit of children.

2. The application of the *liturgical reform* has given birth in Rio to a Higher Institute of Pastoral Liturgy which, notably through its summer session, provides priests and religious with

143

a liturgical formation that cannot but benefit the quality of commentaries in future preaching.

3. The decisive improvement is expected from the renewal of *teaching in the seminaries*. Appreciable efforts are underway, notably at the interdiocesan seminary of the northeast (near Récife), and at the interreligious seminaries of São Paulo and Belo Horizonte. The National Conference of Bishops (CNBB) has authorized the creation of a Higher Pastoral Institute for Vocations, but its objective is centered on the recruiting of priests. Finally, we should cite the several Pastoral Institutes directed by religious which endeavor to complete the pastoral formation received at the seminary.

Sessions and congresses of pastoral orientation have experienced an extraordinary awakening in Brazil since Vatican Council II, both on the national level, under the coordination of a General Secretary of the CNBB and its departments, and on the level of the Eleven Ecclesiastical Regions, in unequal fashion. We might mention in this area:

1. A "Project for Evangelization" within whose framework one should "reflect and elaborate, theologically and pastorally, on the message to be transmitted and the basic lines of a missionary activity"; set in motion by a National Seminary in February 1966, it will be concluded by another in February 1970.

2. A series of regional courses, of some ten days each, looking toward the formation of regional leaders in the priestly ministry, who will then transmit the elements of renewal to the priests of each region.

3. The official Center of Socio-Religious Studies (CERES) is charged with conducting a survey of the present state of missionary preaching from August 1967 to August 1969.

The printed tools used by priests run the risk of appearing still insufficient. The only review on an international level published in Brazil in the field that concerns us, *Rivista Eclesiástica Brasileira,* reaches the priests in the country and assuredly helps in theologico-liturgical information. It used to publish plans for sermons but discontinued that practice; its chronicles are always more widely read than its in-depth articles. Other less important reviews exist on different levels. Foreign publications scarcely reach any but specialists, except for the Portuguese edition of *Concilium* which has gotten off to a good start.

The vehicles of the Catholic dailies and the radio seem to be still suffering from a conception of the "Catholic truth" as "apologetic truth", which no longer corresponds to the exigencies of culturally evolving milieux. We are hoping that, somewhere in between the organs of the neutral press and the maladroitly hyperconfessional organs, groups of the laity will dare to place their responsibility and freedom at the service of information which imposes respect on all by virtue of its openness and objectivity.

We might also mention two important problems having to do with priests: (1) Though popular works are now plentiful in Portuguese, this is not the case with more technical studies indispensable for a deeper renewal in any area. Outside of specialists, few Brazilian priests read works in foreign languages. (2) Priests engaged in the ministry in Brazil let themselves be so carried away by action that they no longer tolerate more than the most restricted readings in extent and profundity.

Instead of having acquired an easy familiarity with the homogeneous theology of the conciliar documents, often a superficial reading is given them and this serves to buttress attitudes which were picked up elsewhere. Preaching itself thus reveals great numbers of priests in Latin America who may be generally classed under either of two extreme types: (1) conservative priests, often pastors of bourgeois parishes, whose preaching is systematically asocial and disincarnate or devoted to the defense of the status quo in every domain; (2) liberal priests more in touch with a youth that reacts against moralizing and static formalism, but risks basing itself on the Council for innovations that can be contested. This adds fuel to an excessive tension between two wings of Brazilian Christianity; its resolution, we believe, must be sought in a careful examination of all points of view rather than in the hardening of authoritative measures.

There is one last characteristic of Brazilian preaching we should mention. It will more and more pass from the hands of the priests, who are relatively small in number, and be entrusted to *religious* to whom parishes without priests are progressively being entrusted and to married *deacons* who will enjoy an analogous mission.

Juan Ochagavía, S.J. /*Santiago, Chile*

Preaching in Chile

In Chile the life of the Catholic Church is a kind of halfway house between Christendom and the foreign missions. Approximately 80% of the population have their children baptized, but religious instruction is gravely deficient and Sunday Mass attendance, insofar as that can be taken as a criterion of Christian life, is on average less than 15% of Catholics. Hence for the last five years the pastoral plan of the bishops has placed the emphasis on evangelization.

In recent years the most notable effort in this field has been the "general missions" held in every diocese of the country, starting in 1963. These, unlike the traditional form of mission, did not limit themselves to the renewal of the Christian in his individual life and reception of the sacraments. Their principal aim was the proclamation and teaching of the Gospel to groups, either of family members or of neighbors, trying in this way to form more vital Christian communities. The secondary aim of the general mission was to establish a presence of Christians in the construction of the world, a task of unspeakable urgency throughout the South American continent. The general mission was directed by an integrated team of priests, nuns and laity, but the leading role was played by the people evangelized who took an extremely active part in every meeting, conference and inquiry on religion. This system of active cooperation and dialogue demanded a special training for the missionaries, of which the main result was a much closer contact with the people, still manifest even today in many parts of the country both in catechesis and in ordinary preaching.

A 1964 survey in the city of Santiago by the bishop's Bureau of Religious Sociology gives us some valuable data on preaching at Sunday Mass. Taking as a basis the analysis of the preaching at ninety Masses, a representative sample of the city, they obtained the following picture. The average length of the sermon was twelve minutes. In twenty-two cases (26%) the preacher did not speak Spanish clearly, with a proportionate loss of attention and interest among his listeners. This is due in part to the fact that, given the scarcity of Chilean clergy, many of these priests are foreigners, and also in part to difficulties of acoustics, which were deficient in 19% of cases. In 83.6% of cases it was noted that the sermon had been prepared and not improvised; the ideas were clear and well expressed (78.7%) and the structure simple and well planned (80%). About 60% of the preachers centered their sermon on the person of Christ, and only 5% of the sermons were negatively moralizing.

With regard to the listeners' reaction, only 48.5% showed any interest in the sermon. Perhaps this is due to the fact that only 52% of preachers seemed to have a good contact with their audience, 18% an adequate one and 30% a defective one. Among the causes for this lack of communication are mentioned language difficulties and the excessive abstraction of many sermons—they did not seem to have many roots in real life or much practical bearing on it (41.1%). Another recent survey (May 1967) indicates that this difficulty on the part of the faithful still exists; the majority think that preaching, even if in itself well prepared and lucid, lacks realism and means little to them as a source of inspiration and Christian strength in their daily lives. A proof of this lies in the fact that many find it too lengthy, even though objectively it lasts no longer than ten to twelve minutes.

In order to help priests prepare and improve their sermons, the Preaching Department of the National Episcopate sends them a series of aids in leaflet form, prepared by pastors and scriptural experts, for the Sunday or feastday homily. The aim of these leaflets is clearly defined and limited; no "schemes" are offered on which to hang a second-hand homily, but rather a solid foundation on which to prepare it. Consequently, there is no question of taking the place of the irreplaceable personal reflection of each pastor but rather of stimulating and leading it to a concrete application of the Word of God for his particular flock here and now. Each leaflet has two parts, the first of *doctrinal orientation,* which expounds the overall doctrinal sense of the biblical readings, and the second of *pastoral orientation,* which tries to give a practical application that the pastor has to adapt to the mentality of his hearers.

In Chile there is no review specifically concerned with the problem of preaching. The monthly publication *Pastoral Popular* only partially fulfills this purpose, mostly because its interests are broader than preaching as such.

Certain factors are making an indirect contribution to the renewal of preaching, factors that must have enduring but rather long-term effects. Among them may be mentioned the days of *aggiornamento* for the clergy, held since Vatican Council II in every diocese. Out of these have arisen various isolated initiatives, such as Bible study groups of priests and laymen to examine and prepare the Sunday sermons. Beginning in April 1968 a Pastoral Institute for the whole country will begin to function in Santiago; its aim will be to offer priests, religious and laymen an opportunity of renewing themselves, in a more systematic way, in dogmatic, homiletic, moral and pastoral theology, thus corresponding with the wish of Vatican Council II to see a continuous process of formation throughout a Christian's life.

The catechetical and liturgical renewals by themselves are factors that are bound to have a notable influence on the improvement of preaching. Finally, the diocesan synods, countrywide as from 1967, are bound to show more clearly the real way to tackle the problem of preaching and without doubt will be in a position to offer more realistic solutions worked out with the collaboration of all Catholics.

Daniel Morrisey, O.P. / *Dubuque, Iowa*

Catholic Preaching in the United States, England and the English-Speaking World

The renewal of Catholic preaching in the United States is marked with the characteristics of the American Church: youth and vigor, a concern for contemporary social issues promoted by the use of the most modern communications techniques, a new but indelibly ecumenical spirit, and a growing need and appreciation of scholarship.

American Catholic homiletic thought first showed signs of new life in 1935. *The Homiletic and Pastoral Review* offered to a large readership sermon outlines and suggestions from the best-known Canadian, British Commonwealth and American preachers. The Preachers' Institute at Catholic University in Washington, D.C., was influential in the training of preachers. Msgr. (now Bishop) Fulton J. Sheen preached coast-to-coast on radio's "The Catholic Hour". After World War II, however, the situation had changed completely: *The Homiletic and Pastoral Review* deemphasized homiletics; the parish mission was facing a crisis; Bishop Sheen was still popular, but his weekly television show was a series of widely diversified talks, not preaching.

These conditions led in 1956 and 1957 to the exploratory discussions which provided the foundation for the Catholic Homiletic Society (CHS).[1] This organization, still the only one

[1] The Catholic Homiletic Society, 4453 McPherson Avenue, St. Louis, Missouri 63108.

of its kind, has led the renewal of preaching in the American Catholic Church. Membership in the CHS has grown from seventy charter members to more than 1,300 in the United States and English-speaking Canada, including priests, Protestant ministers, seminarians, and laymen whose professions involve them in the training of future preachers.

The CHS is very active—not only in its attempts to combine homiletics with professional training in speech, but also in developing ways of improving and renewing homiletic scholarship. To men directly engaged in preaching it offers immediate, practical help in six ways:

1. 10,400 English speaking priests receive *The Homiletic Service*[2] edited by the Catholic Centre of Saint Paul University in Ottawa, Canada. This monthly publication contains homily outlines for Sundays, holydays, Lenten Masses and special occasions (e.g., marriage, funeral, graduation), and also offers a series of outlines for conferences for religious.

2. The CHS publishes a monthly ten-page *Newsletter,* containing comment on recent publications, experiments in preaching and new ideas. Information in the *Newsletter* from a Lutheran (Missouri Synod) professor of speech in St. Louis on how to set up a videotape laboratory to train seminarians led to the installation of videotape equipment at the Aquinas Institute (Roman Catholic) in Dubuque, Iowa, where it is shared with the Theological Seminary of the University of Dubuque (United Presbyterian, U.S.A.) and Wartburg Theological Seminary (American Lutheran Church).

3. In January, 1966, the CHS launched a new ecumenical journal of homiletics, *Preaching.* Although there are several excellent Protestant journals devoted to sermons (*The Pulpit* and *Pulpit Digest* among others), neither Catholics nor Protestants have ever concerned themselves exclusively with the theory and practice behind the writing of sermons. *Preaching* does not publish sermons, but it offers new approaches, both theoretical and practical, to the homiletic. A recent issue followed a theme

2 *The Homiletic Service,* 1 Stewart Street, Ottawa 2, Canada.

centering around the incorporation of dialogue into preaching and the growing awareness of the need for active participation on the part of congregations for a fully effective communication. The pastor of an inner city parish described his experiences with the dialogue homily, while another author used the documents of Vatican Council II, based upon tradition, to offer the dialogue homily a theoretical justification. Another pair of articles described the successful use of a team of trained laywomen in retreats and investigated historically and theologically the question of laymen as preachers.

4. To stimulate the sharing of scholarly research in homiletics, the CHS sponsors serious studies such as *Recent Homiletical Thought: A Bibliography, 1935–1965* (Abingdon Press, 1967). Here can be found an annotated appraisal of all books (443), articles (1080) and theses (609) that have appeared in English during the past 30 years. The work is co-edited by Dr. William Thompson, professor of homiletics at Eastern Baptist Theological Seminary, Philadelphia, and Father William Toohey of Holy Cross College, Washington, D.C., who together edit the book review section of *Preaching*.

5. During the summer of 1967, five Preachers' Workshops were conducted across the United States by the CHS in Kansas, Illinois, Minnesota, Missouri and California. These five-day in-service training sessions included study of the theology of preaching, emotional writing and preaching, voice production and contemporary preaching problems.

6. The pattern of steady growth of the CHS is evident in the increasing attendance at its annual three-day convention. Among speakers at the 1967 convention in Hollywood was a Lutheran minister who explained his plan for "single image projection", in which photographs are handed to each person in a congregation as a visual image upon which the preacher then centers his sermon. A Paulist priest spoke on the psychology of the American listener from his experience as producer of a TV theological theater series with a yearly audience estimated at 150 million. Special attention is also given to the "Cursillo" movement

and to the widespread experimentation in small-group retreats stressing religious experience.

In England there is no organized effort to better Catholic preaching, nor are there publications specializing in homiletics. The Church of England since 1960 has sponsored the College of Preachers in London.[3] This College, much like the Anglican Preachers' College in Washington, D.C., conducts week-long refresher courses for small groups of priests who have been ordained ten to fifteen years. More than 1,000 Anglican priests have taken this program, which concentrates more upon the techniques of preaching than upon a rethinking of the homiletic. The Preachers' College is not yet an ecumenical effort.

[3] The College of Preachers, 4 Cambridge Place, London W8, England.

Heinz Schuster/*Saarbrücken, W. Germany*
Karlheinz Hoffmann, S.J./*Frankfurt, W. Germany*

Mass Media and Proclamation

I

THE PRACTICAL THEOLOGICAL ASPECTS OF THE PROBLEM

Apparently the Church is no longer able to find her way about as easily in the sphere of communications provided by modern society as she was in the sphere of communications that existed in the past. Throughout her history, in carrying out her task of proclaiming the Word of God either to those who already believed or to those in the world who did not yet believe, she has always known how to make use of the existing sphere of human communications as well as the existing means of communication, to a very great extent without hesitating and without theorizing too much. The primitive Church first availed herself of the traditional community of master and disciples and then very rapidly evolved—within the framework of the world to which her mission was directed—the use of itinerant preachers and the epistle. The early missionaries relied upon extensive personal communication which they exploited by following the paths of economic, political and military traffic.

The invention of printing and particularly of the film and of radio, however, brought about a decisive change in the structure of the sphere of human communications. The *medium* of communication was created and thereby the possibility of a medial information or proclamation addressed to an indefinite number of readers, viewers or listeners.

An historical heritage may play some part in the Church's dilemma with regard to the modern media of communications —the mass medium of the press was initially dominated by a liberalism that was hostile to the Church. This meant that these new media helped to disseminate the ideas, theories and ideologies of groups which had, up to that time, not been able to exert much influence within human society, whereas there was not a corresponding number of preachers in the Church to do the same work. The modern mass media made it possible for one individual—and the "political" power of these media is ultimately based on this—to reach an unlimited number of readers, listeners, viewers or spectators and to inform, influence and even form them, insofar as that individual has control over that medium.

In principle and in theory, the earlier conflict of the Church's pastoral care and the reticence of the Church's official leadership with regard to the modern media of communications belong to the past. However, this does not mean that the problem has been solved for the Church and her theology. The mass media have, in the meantime, achieved an unforeseen level of development and power. The media themselves have become extensively institutionalized. In other words, the various social groups have created laws, principles, authoritative bodies and legal constitutions which provide, on the one hand, the social norms and the support for these media and, on the other hand, the guarantee of the maintenance of human freedom and of man's right to relevant "neutral" information and so on. The Church's official contribution to this phase of the institutionalization of the mass media has been very slight or else—in view of Vatican Council II's *Decree on the Media of Social Communications*—it has come too late.

It is precisely here that practical theology becomes interested. In accordance with its essential task of reflecting about how the work of proclaiming the Church may be accomplished today, it is confronted with the following questions.

1. How far is man's present situation, and above all how far

is his sphere of communications, already determined and nor-
malized by the modern mass media?

2. How far, in fact, does a large part (from the quantitative
point of view) of the Church's proclamation take place through
these media, either by the Church being the passive object of
secular discussion which is bound to take place through these
media, or by individual representatives of the Church proclaiming the Christian message, imparting theological information and
so on (which is in fact what happens) with the help of these
media?

3. How far is a greater part both of the Christian community
and also and above all of non-Christian society already reached
by this "extraordinary" form of medial proclamation?

4. How far is this "extraordinary" medial proclamation, at
least from the point of view of its scope and quantity, more effective and far-reaching than the "ordinary" proclamation that
has, up to the present, been almost exclusively applied within
the Christian community—that is, catechesis and preaching?

5. How far is the content of the Gospel and of the Church's
dogmas and moral teaching factually modified by the nature and
structure of the modern mass media, or how far are the demands
for some modification of this kind that these media unques-
tionably make at all thought out?

However rough and provisional the formulation of these questions may be, it will be obvious that the answers given to them
will to a very great extent determine how the Church is to function most effectively in the future, or at least how we are, within
the various disciplines of practical theology, to think about the
Church of the future. A few theologumena or pastoral principles
which are bound to be affected by our answers to these questions are given below.

1. Is the Church's proclamation (her testimony to God's acts
for the salvation of mankind) at all possible with the help of
these media, if the frequently made assertion that this proclamation is to be defined as a "personal encounter" or an "act of
personal communication" is true?

2. Do the accomplishments of the Church within the framework of this medial communication really amount less to a strict "proclamation of the Gospel" than to an act in which the Church simply presents herself and provides information about questions of general religiosity and morality?

3. If a positive answer is given to the first question, is the Church's traditional type of missionary activity and the personal effort and financial expense involved in this still in any way meaningful when compared with the possibilities offered by the modern mass media? Should all the Church's financial resources and all her theological, didactic and rhetorical efforts not be directed, for example, toward a worldwide "mission of the air", using only very few transmitting stations?

4. Again, if a positive answer is given to the first question, is it not clear evidence of faulty planning in the Christian countries when, on the one hand, very small parishes still have their own priest while, on the other hand, it is still a very rare occurrence for priests to be made freely available to devote themselves to the many tasks and possibilities offered by the press, radio and television? Is the same faulty planning not also evident in the training of priests, which is to a very great extent still based on the assumption that there is only one "means" of communication today, the pulpit of the parish church?

5. Is it still possible for the truth of Christianity to be formulated and handed on in language that is intelligible only to the initiated (who were brought up on the catechism), although in fact an increasingly large number of "outsiders" and "uninitiated" people also hear this message whenever a representative of the Church makes use of one or other of the mass media?

II

THE PRESENT TASK OF PRACTICAL THEOLOGY

In view of the questions and problems outlined above, one might well be tempted to call for a kind of "theology of social communication". Without going into the theoretical problems that would be raised by a demand of this kind, the following points are put forward for consideration. Social communication and the present media of this communication are, quite simply, a fact. Our own era is furthermore characterized by certain features that are above all determined by the existence of radio and television. (a) The sphere of communications open to the individual is practically the whole world. (b) All relevant opinions, truths, ideologies, religions and so on are discussed in this worldwide dialogue. This means that the Church cannot, even if she wanted to, any longer remain outside this worldwide discussion. (c) The media of communications themselves have already become highly organized on almost all continents and in individual countries, and transmitting rights, licenses, wavelengths and so on have already been widely granted or disposed of. This means that the Church would not be able to put a completely new practice into effect even if it were based on the most perfect theory (or theology).

In other words, all theory or theology that is concerned with the present-day media of communications must recognize and accept these basic concepts if it is to avoid being pure theory and thus the very opposite of Christian theology. As a result, the development of these media has led to the formulation of certain definite understandings and practical principles which must be recognized and accepted and cannot be elaborated beforehand.

This, then, is the broad outline, in principle, of the task facing practical theology. It was quite clear to the editors, at the very first consultation held to discuss the theme and contents of this article, that it was no longer possible to deal with the question of the Church's preaching and her proclamation of the Christian message without at the same time also talking about the mass media or the so-called medial "proclamation". In view of this, the authors from the very outset dismissed all thought of writing an article based on the principles of general pastoral theology which would, in the long run, simply have amounted to a summary of Vatican Council II's *Decree on the Media of Social Communications*. It seemed to be far more meaningful and necessary to investigate and analyze the extent to which a medial proclamation was in fact already being carried out today by the Church. Going further, there was also a real need to attempt to find an answer to other, related questions. For example, was this medial proclamation thought of either as a real "proclamation of the Gospel" or simply as the imparting of information by the Church? Was it above all directed toward the community of believers among the listeners and viewers or toward those outside the believing community? Was it based on an official institution of the Church in each country or was it—in the sense of "extraordinary" pastoral care—simply carried out by individual priests or theologians?

Anyone who is to any extent familiar with the intimate workings of the mass media (and we are here thinking in the first place only of radio and television) will know at once that the fact referred to is subject to enormous differences and that very detailed and extensive research is required if any foundation is to be laid for a conception of and a strategy in practical theology, both of which are becoming increasingly necessary. Whether the Church's proclamation and pastoral care are suitably adapted to mankind and the world of the future is to a great extent dependent on whether the Church will succeed in incorporating the future sphere and media of human communications into her pastoral planning.

III

DETAILED QUESTIONS RESULTING
FROM AN ANALYSIS OF THE SITUATION

We provide below a brief survey of the detailed questions arising from the research which was conceived and commenced some time ago in connection with this article, but which could not, as might well be expected, be concluded before the article went to press. This survey cannot hope to yield a result when in reality no result exists. It can only indicate the concrete problem and the differences within it, a problem which continues to exist after every investigation, however extensive, and one which can never be "solved", but only clarified.

1. To what extent does the Church as a socially relevant group in any given country have her own radio or television programs or her own stations? Does she share these programs or stations? Does she own her own stations or have her own frequencies for transmission?

2. What is the legal and social constitution of the existing broadcasting station? Is it in the hands of a commercial undertaking? Is it maintained by all the relevant groups in society? Is it controlled by the government?

3. What kind of "presence of the Church" has, in the media of radio and television, been tried out and been most successful up to the present time: (a) the sermon bearing witness to the Christian faith (in practice, an extension of the Sunday sermon in the parish "on the air"); (b) information about the Christian faith (in the manner of an "educational" lecture or talk); (c) open discussion with representatives of other religious communities or with non-Christians; (d) spiritual or moral encouragement (in the sense of pre-Christian help in life); (e) documentation from the life of the Church; (f) religious films or plays?

4. What financial resources and what staff are available: (a) for consultation and planning what to do with the times of transmission that are in fact at the Church's disposal; (b) for experiments of a technical, artistic and didactic nature; (c) for the initial and further training of the younger staff?

5. Is information about the Church, her life and her teaching restricted to the "Church's" times of transmission or is information from the world of the religious communities also given in the general news programs? If the latter, is any mention made in such news programs of the comments, attitudes, etc. of the Church authorities?

6. If subjects—the discussion of which would, because of the very nature of these subjects, normally involve the participation of a member of the Church or even the taking up of a definite position on his part—are dealt with in general programs (such as discussions), is it customary for a representative of the Church to take part, or is it in principle not customary, but possible for this to happen?

7. What theological or Church themes are in fact preferred and which are the easiest to carry out: (a) those dealing with teaching about the faith; (b) those dealing with moral teaching; (c) those connected with the "life of the Church"; (d) those connected with "Christian life"; (e) those dealing with the history of the Church; (f) those taken from hagiography; (g) scriptural subjects; (h) those taken from any other sphere?

8. Are the religious communities accorded regular times of transmission (in a definite rotation) or are they given a hearing: (a) as the occasion arises; (b) as a fixed theme; (c) only on feast days?

9. Is the confessional aspect of the Christian Churches given any real opportunity to express itself in the media of communications? Are restrictions in fact always imposed in connection with the emphasis given to the confessional character of a religious community? Are any statistics available concerning the reaction of the listeners and viewers who have demanded these "restrictions"?

IV

ONE MODEL AMONG MANY

The following brief outline of broadcasting in the Federal Republic of Western Germany can be given. It will not provide an answer to all the detailed questions that are set out above, but it can be regarded as an example of a description of the existing situation in one country.

The whole broadcasting system in Western Germany is neither commercially based nor State-owned. Its structure is rather like that of the B.B.C. in that it is a legally established public body. In other words, each of the so-called socially relevant groups, including the Churches, has about one representative member on the controlling bodies of the individual radio and television stations—the bodies, that is, which bear ultimate responsibility (and in two of the twelve broadcasting stations, this representation takes place via the political parties). This structure thus provides at the very outset an opportunity for information of a religious nature to be given a definite form in the programs.

It is only to the religious groups (there are 26.8 million Catholics among the total West German population of 59.3 million) that regular special broadcasting times are conceded. As far as television is concerned, these times are partly allocated on a "biconfessional" basis (in 1967, in the first of two television programs at a national level, this part was about 16%). Otherwise, however, the times are divided between the two confessions in such a way that they in practice either alternate or are shared, the Catholic Church receiving thus about 50% of the total time for religious broadcasting. The programs are planned and produced by special departments or by editors especially appointed for this task in the broadcasting stations and also financed by the stations themselves. The Church collaborates in this planning and production in a consultative capacity—priests are especially appointed for this task—and this collaboration is partly regulated by law. The priests appointed to each station receive their salary from the Church. These priests and the representatives of the Church on the controlling bodies form, subject to the guidance of priests especially authorized by the bishops, the governing bodies of the Church's work in radio and television. These governing bodies plan the Church's collaboration and actively supervise the structure of the whole sector of broadcasting. The departments for radio and television are at the center of this work and a special press institute is set apart for the task of critically assessing radio and television programs.

As far as sound broadcasting is concerned, the number of religious programs in the whole of broadcasting, spread over all the different stations, has been estimated at an average of about 1.4%, allowing for a density of about 18.2 million wireless receivers (on December 31, 1966) among 59.3 million inhabitants. A good fifth of this time is taken up with broadcast religious services, mostly on Sundays (Mass, services of the Word and to some extent special services for the sick). Another fifth is devoted to the treatment of religious topics in the form of lectures or talks for adults (there is relatively little of this material for children within the framework of school broadcasting). Approximately another fifth of the time is used for talks on weekday mornings, lasting about five minutes, and broadcast before the beginning of the working day. A further fifth of the total time is devoted to news and commentary and a final fifth to miscellaneous subjects such as discussions about books.

The predominating forms of "reporting" and "documentation" play a relatively small part in religious broadcasting. There is no religious radio drama—the Church's departments for radio and television do not consider that this is justified—and there is no listener research. It would seem that the short morning talks have a relatively good following. A rather avant-garde spirit—if it is permissible to use this word—has prevailed for some time in the discussion of religious topics in the form of lectures and talks. Otherwise, Catholic broadcasting is discreetly concerned with giving religious programs an attractive form. In the sense outlined above, the Church's share in broadcasting suffers from a severe shortage of staff and finance. Apart from making rather amateurish attempts to try out various people in front of the microphone, there is hardly any real training for free-lance collaborators and priests.

As far as television is concerned, there is a density of 12.7 million sets (on December 31, 1966), and a distinction has to be made here between two separate programs on the national level—the federal program on the one hand, and the central program on the other.[1]

The first program (ARD) provides a number of religious broadcasts, amounting to about 1.4% of the whole program. Televised religious services (the Mass) only take place on the three main feasts of the Church year. An evening service, lasting about half an hour, is broadcast on one Sunday every month, alternating with the Protestants, at 5:15 in the evening. Again alternating with the Protestants, a priest speaks for five minutes every Sunday night at about 10 o'clock on a program known as the "Word for Sunday". This address is conceived as an "open meditation" with a Christian content, and confessional differences are generally kept in the background. It is watched by about 30 to 35% of the viewers. There is also a half-hour program, again alternating with the Protestants, at 11:30 every Sunday morning. This takes the form of a documentary or a report about events and developments within the life of the Church or of religious interest and about the lives of prominent religious personalities. The aim is to stimulate thought or to encourage viewers to commitment. This program is watched by about 6 to 9% of the viewers. Four times a year, topical questions of religious interest are discussed in this first, federal program. About once every two months, there is a puppet play for children in the afternoon, based on a "story" from the Old Testament.

The second television program (ZDF) also provides a number of religious broadcasts, amounting in this case to about 2.1% of the total program. Again, religious services are televised only on the three main feasts. There is also an evening service of thirty minutes' duration, alternating with the Protestants and watched by about 5 to 8% of the viewers. This corresponds to the similar broadcast on the first program, but is shown every Sunday at 6:30 in the evening. Every second Monday night at 10 p.m., viewers can see fifteen minutes of the "Diary of the

---

[1] There is also a third type of program—the regional program—but this is not considered here because of the lack of audience research.

Catholic Church", containing news and brief reports—usually topical—on Catholic life. About 6 to 8% of the viewers watch this program.

On both television programs, a certain amount of space is also given, in the half-hour transmissions, to news about the life of the Church in neighboring and in missionary countries as well as to themes connected with help for underdeveloped countries. There are hardly any talks or discussions during this second program, although these do take place from time to time on the general evening program. There is an almost complete absence of programs with the theme of ecumenical contact between the confessions or ecumenical cooperation. There is also no specialized technical training for free-lance collaborators or priests. The Church's representatives in the television service are overburdened by a lack of resources. The aim of all these religious programs, both on radio and on television, is to enable Catholics, whether they are active members of the Church or not, to take part in this way in the life of the Church. What is aimed at in the religious programs is a quality both in form and in content corresponding to that of the other radio and television broadcasts and in accordance with the conditions imposed by a country that is divided between Catholic and Protestant and also rather widely divergent from the religious point of view.

Within the framework of the possibilities offered, as long as the training of future priests and lay people to work in the mass media, the conditions of work of the Church's representatives on the various broadcasting bodies and coordination between all concerned can be improved, there are many clear opportunities for the proclamation of the Christian message to be adapted in form and content to radio and television, especially in connection with the reporting and discussion of topical events and developments. Technical assistance and support in the program sector for the proclamation by radio and television of the message in the underdeveloped and missionary countries might, moreover, be entirely lacking at the very outset because of a shortage of personnel and insufficient financial resources. We are still too little aware of our international duty here. Let us hope that the "World Assembly for the Means of Social Communication" arouses a sense of responsibility among men that is commensurate with the importance of the mass media.

PART III
DOCUMENTATION
CONCILIUM

Office of the Executive Secretary
Nijmegen, Netherlands

Concilium General Secretariat/*Nijmegen, Netherlands*

Introduction to Documentation

The aim of the Documentation section of *Concilium* is *not* to collect topical *facts* but topical *ideas*. Theology can only live where ideas develop and mature. This is one of the reasons why theology is essentially historical, and this holds especially true for pastoral theology. If we take the historical character of this theology seriously, we have to ask ourselves how far convictions that have developed historically in a Christian culture can be integrated into a culture which has not yet been penetrated by the values of the Good News. Within the Christian culture, the value of the monogamous marriage has become obvious, to the degree that we are not always conscious of the fact that this is the fruit of a laborious effort. The historical character of this value acutely affects the missionary who has grown up in a system of—for him obvious —theological values, but is now confronted with a culture and social structures where polygamy is equally self-evident as a value. Is it then the missionary's task to oppose one value with another, or would he be justified in pleading with pastoral prudence for a transition phase where the social structures are first penetrated by Christian values so that he then can put forward the Christian ideal of a monogamous marriage as a human reality and as something that is fully viable within the context of Christian salvation?

171

Such a question demands scientific reflection since the solution is not exactly easy. Mission work, indeed, is not merely the converting of individual persons to the fullness of the Gospel but also the Christianization of structures.

With this in mind [1] the American missionary in Africa, E. Hillman, approaches this complicated problem without reaching a definite conclusion. To discuss this problem, however, shows respect for other cultures and for the conviction that the days of a spiritual colonialism are gone.

[1] K. Rahner, A. Darlap, *et al., Sacramentum Mundi* I (Freiburg i. Br., 1967), p. 996: "It is therefore understandable that marriage can never be looked at as an isolated affair between two partners, but always as an integral part of the universally human, supraindividual, ethical and religious context, and as ordered toward the family, so that in law, in morals and as an ethical norm this view has always been given priority over the requirements of marriage as such."

Eugene Hillman, C.S.Sp./*Monduli, Tanzania*

Polygyny Reconsidered

This article is offered as a preliminary basis for discussing the problem of evangelization in areas where simultaneous polygyny is regarded as an indispensable socio-economic institution and cultural ideal. What is presented here is neither a comprehensive treatment of the question nor a definitive answer. This is simply an effort to indicate the present dimensions of the problem, and to suggest some possible approaches which might lead to a new solution. The intention is, therefore, to show both the urgency and the possibility of fully reconsidering this matter in the light of some further sociological, historical, biblical, theological and ecclesiological reflection.

The word "polygyny" (as distinguished from the more general term "polygamy") here refers specifically to a widely recognized and socially valid form of permanent marriage in which a man may have more than one wife simultaneously.

A Missionary Question

A missionary, working in an area where polygyny is the prevailing and socially integrated system of marriage, is apt to be seen as one who comes to break up the natural family unity and to shatter the existing complex of marriage-related human bonds which serve both the economic interests and the social unity of a whole community. In such a situation the missionary hardly appears as one who comes to introduce the sacramental sign of human unity, and the positive law of monogamy is apt to be regarded as more fundamental than, or at least identical with, the Gospel leaven of faith and hope and love. Yet the aim of the Church is to incarnate herself among all peoples as the universal sign of mankind's unity, and the New Testament *kerygma* is clearly not identical with the law of monogamy.

The Gospel leaven may be fully activated among believers only through their explicit participation in the sacramental life of the Church. The aims and ideals of the Christian vocation cannot otherwise be attained. A non-baptized person, who in good faith had already accepted the social obligations of a polygynous marriage, should not therefore be expected to have actually attained the Christian ideal of marriage even before he has had any possibility of participating in the sacramental life of the Church. Yet this is precisely what is required of him when the practice of monogamy is insisted upon as a necessary pre-condition (on a level of importance with faith) for baptism. "Having begun with the Spirit", the missionary message thus "ends with the flesh" in such a way that what is finally decisive is not faith, but law (cf. Gal. 3, 2–5).

In this traditional missionary approach, the law of monogamy (in the most literal and legalistic sense) tends to be identified in practice with the New Testament *kerygma*; external conformity to a legal prescription then becomes so overwhelmingly important, and finally decisive in practice, that it may even be a sub-stitute for the real conversion of faith which alone sets a man on the long and difficult road that leads only gradually to the Chris-tian ideal of conduct in every aspect of his life. In this way also the explicit Gospel teaching concerning the primacy of love and the indissolubility of marriage is rendered secondary. A man is told, in the name of the Christian ideal of marriage and family life, that he must *divorce* the mother of his own children.

This legalistic procedure is, moreover, notorious in its lack of Christian consideration for the unfortunate women who are "sent away". Their previously contracted conjugal rights, their social status, and even their relationships with their own children are simply ignored, and it is not always easy, or even possible, for them to become wives again. Many of them must choose to live either like nuns or like prostitutes. Their fate is determined by the structures of the secular society in which they live. It is sometimes a cruel fate.

More often than not, however, the members of polygynous societies—precisely because this legal condition is both intolerable and incomprehensible—are unable to respond fully to the call of Christ. The message of Christian freedom does not finally liberate them, because it is presented equivocally under the burden of a law (cf. Acts 15, 10).

So it is that the work of evangelizing is highly problematical, and sometimes quite impossible, among peoples for whom polygyny is a normal practice and an ideal custom. Before deciding that the fault is all theirs, it might be well first to question the soundness of the practical attitudes, the biblical interpretations and the theological suppositions that have characterized the traditional Christian approach to this particular missionary problem.

Sociological Aspects

On the basis of the available data, the following general estimates are made concerning the extent to which polygyny is practiced among the indigenous peoples of sub-Saharan Africa.[1] There are about 150 wives for every 100 husbands. The mean number of wives per married man is about 1.5, and the ratio of married women to married men is about 3 to 2. As a reasonable generalization it may be said that about 35 percent of all married men are polygynous. The evidence suggests also that, while the practice of polygyny has decreased among some of these

[1] Cf. V. Dorjahn, "The Factor of Polygyny in African Demography," in *Continuity and Change in African Cultures*, edited by W. Boscom and M. Herskovits (Chicago, 1959), pp. 87–112. See also E. Nida, *Custom, Culture and Christianity* (London, 1963), p. 105.

peoples, it has increased among others; thus it is assumed that
the overall situation has remained relatively unchanged during
the past forty years.[2] Whatever might be said about the precise
accuracy of the available data, it is obvious that polygyny is
still a widespread custom in this part of the world, and it will
continue to be so for some time to come.[3]

In many societies polygyny is required by customary law as
a form of social security for a widow (and her children) whose
conjugal rights become the responsibility of the brother of a
deceased husband. But polygyny is generally practiced only
where there is a surplus of marriageable-age women in relation
to marriageable-age men. Such a surplus is due to a combina-
tion of factors which, variable and debatable as they may be,
tend to produce a female predominance in most countries south
of the Sahara.[4]

The major reason for a surplus of marriageable-age women,
however, is the notable discrepancy in the chronological ages
of men and women when they actually get married. Women
marry relatively early in life, while men marry relatively late.
The reasons for this are numerous, mixed and variable. In every
society in the world the appropriate marriageable-ages of men
and women are determined by customs and ideals which are
profoundly rooted in history, economy, traditional beliefs, notions of prestige, concepts of decency, etc.

Closer analysis suggests that the extent of polygyny is determined more by economic considerations than by anything else
—although not in isolation from everything else that constitutes
the total cultural fabric of a society in which polygyny is practiced. A man would normally be considered of marriageable-
age, for example, only when he had acquired the minimum
wealth required in his society for the support of a family, and

[2] Cf. V. Dorjahn, op. cit., pp. 100f.
[3] Those who believe that the socio-economic condition of the masses
is changing rapidly in sub-Saharan Africa should read René Dumont,
False Start in Africa (London, 1966), a translation of L'Afrique Noire
est Mal Partie (Paris, 1962).
[4] Cf. V. Dorjahn, op. cit., pp. 105ff.

this would depend very much upon the economic resources and opportunities available to him where he lives. There is also the problem of paying the so-called "bride-price", which may be a formidable obstacle to the marriage of young men in certain areas. While this widespread custom lends stability to the institution of marriage and helps to maintain the bonds of indissolubility, it also makes it difficult for men to marry at an early age.

The norms of a productive and cash-economy society are completely irrelevant to peoples who are still bound to the social structures of a traditional subsistence economy. In this connection it appears to be generally true that the introduction of a sound cash-economy, especially in association with the process of urbanization and formal education, will create a new socioeconomic situation in which men are able to marry at an earlier chronological age. Under such conditions polygyny tends to become an economic liability; thus it gradually ceases to be a common practice and a cultural ideal.[5] At the same time it has been observed that such new conditions, while more compatible with monogamy, also encourage adultery, prostitution, concubinage, divorce and the spread of venereal disease.[6]

Sociological and anthropological studies show quite clearly

[5] Cf. E. Nida, *op. cit.*, p. 105; W. Welbourn, *East African Christian* (London, 1965), pp. 127f. But there are exceptions to this generalization: cf. R. Lystad, "Marriage among the Ashanti and the Agni," in *Continuity and Change in African Cultures*, p. 197.

[6] Cf. V. Dorjahn, *op. cit.*, p. 111, n. 60; in the same volume, cf. P. Ottenberg, "The Changing Economic Position of Women among the Afikpo Ibo," p. 221, and J. B. Christensen, "The Adoptive Functions of the Fanti Priesthood," p. 269. There is also an important work on this whole subject by G. Currens and R. Payne, *An Evaluation of the Policy of the Lutheran Church in Liberia on the Baptism of Polygamists* (Mimeograph copy, June 1965), pp. 4–6: The real issue confronting the Church is not the fact of plural marriage, but rather how to deal with the vast grey area of unresolved difficulties in the relationship between men and women who are unmarried or who are so-called monogamists. . . . What does exist between the majority of members [of the Church] are varying degrees of extramarital liaisons—from casual adultery, or temporary taking of a lover while the wife is nursing a child, to covert but established concubinage. Such relationships are . . . almost universally practiced in the Westernized segment of society."

that, far from being just a matter of male lust, the social institution of polygyny has arisen in certain societies as a natural
and reasonable response to a number of basic human needs
which could not be met adequately by the system of monogamy.[7]
Among other things, polygyny may serve to prevent female
prostitution and male promiscuity where there is a surplus of
marriageable-age women. Also, in areas of chronic food shortage,
a mother may have to prolong the period of breast-feeding and
abstain from sexual intercourse during this time simply in order
to provide sufficient food for the child she has already. In this
way the birth of children may be spaced two or more years
apart. In the meantime, male promiscuity (with all its social
implications) may be controlled by the system of polygyny,
while the population increase maintains a relationship with the
availability of food.[8]

In such a socio-economic context, the Christian insistence
on an immediate change from polygyny to monogamy might
very well cause much more harm than good. The marriage system followed in any particular society is a major dynamic element in the orderly functioning of that society. An integrated
marriage system cannot be radically and immediately changed
without at the same time introducing other far-reaching and
perhaps disintegrating changes into the whole social structure
unless such changes are accompanied by vast and harmonious
economic improvements and educational opportunities. It is not
at all certain that the average Christian missionary has either the
mandate or the competence to change social structures that are
not in themselves evil, but are in fact serving good and constructive social purposes.

Historical Aspects

Monogamy was regarded as the normal rule in all of the
societies where Christianity was accepted in apostolic times.
Even among the Jews polygyny was then no longer common.

[7] Cf. L. Luzbetak, S.V.D., *The Church and Cultures* (Techny, 1963),
p. 247.
[8] Cf. V. Dorjahn, *op. cit.,* pp. 109ff.

It is certain that Christianity did not introduce obligatory monogamy into the Greco-Roman world. Before the advent of Christianity, "monogamy prevailed as the only legitimate form of marriage in Greece and Rome".[9] Indeed, it was the principle of the pagan household religion which, in these societies, "provided the basis for the monogamous and essentially indissoluble character of marriage".[10] Even if they had wished to do so, the apostles could hardly have invented and introduced into the Mediterranean world a new system of marriage, any more than they could have invented and introduced a new language. They simply accepted the existing social structures, and then worked to transform these from within through the leaven of the Gospel.

It is not surprising, therefore, that the early Christians and the New Testament writers should have assumed quite naturally that monogamy was the normal, ideal and universal form of marriage. They did not envisage the possibility of Christianity ever being incarnated in a polygynous society, just as they did not consider the significance of the eucharistic feast in a society where bread and wine are unknown, or the meaning of the Good Shepherd in an area where sheep do not exist. Such societies were inconceivable to them. They were able to see the world only in terms of their own socio-cultural experience and historico-geographical limitations. According to Schillebeeckx: "It is evident, especially in the writings of Paul, not only that social structures are experienced 'in the Lord', but also that there is a danger of transforming these social structures into theological realities when they are viewed in an eschatological light. In other words, the biblical ethos of marriage bears clear traces of the prevailing view of the position of women in a society." [11]

Although concubinage was customary among rulers and

[9] Cf. E. Westermarck, *The History of Human Marriage* III (London, 1925), pp. 47ff.

[10] E. Schillebeeckx, O.P., *Marriage: Secular Reality and Saving Mystery* II (London, 1965), p. 7.

[11] *Ibid.*, pp. 203f. See also J. McKenzie, S.J., *Dictionary of the Bible* (Milwaukee, 1965), p. 551: "Marriage was understood by St. Paul according to 'the common conception of the social position of women' in his particular time and place."

wealthy people, monogamy was the generally recognized form of marriage throughout pre-Christian Europe: among the Franco-Germanic peoples, the Anglo-Saxons and the Celts, as well as the Greco-Romans.[12] Thus, in the course of Europe's evangelization, the question of polygyny did not arise on any significantly large scale, and the practice of monogamy was naturally confirmed as the appropriate form of marriage among Christians. Nevertheless, the attitude of the Church toward the customary forms of marriage among these newly evangelized peoples is highly instructive.

For many centuries in all parts of Europe, "Christian marriage was very much the same as that of pagans".[13] At least up until the 9th century, within the various Christian communities of the Roman Empire, "marriages concluded according to the prevailing customs were considered to be valid".[14] This was the case even among the Germanic Christians who regarded marriage as "a contract between two tribes or extended family groups, rather than a contract between the bride and the bridegroom".[15] "Each different tribe had its own marriage customs, and these were strictly observed. . . ." [16]

What the historical evidence shows is that marriage among the earliest Christians in all parts of Europe was understood and accepted by the Church according to the prevailing socio-cultural outlook of the different "tribes and tongues and peoples and nations" whose institutions were only gradually transformed, from within, by the leaven of the Gospel. Marriage was recognized by the Church as "a secular reality set within the framework of all the other secular realities" which make up the total social structure of this or that particular people.[17]

At first glance it would appear that the Council of Trent had settled once and for all any question concerning the possible

---

[12] Cf. E. Westermarck, *op. cit.*
[13] E. Schillebeeckx, *op. cit.* II, p. 18.
[14] *Ibid.*, p. 20.
[15] *Ibid.*, pp. 33f.
[16] *Ibid.*, p. 36.
[17] *Ibid.*, pp. 201f.; Vol. I, p. 21.

compatibility of Christianity with polygyny.[18] But it must be noted that the Council fathers were not concerned with the problem as it arises with reference to the work of evangelization in polygynous societies of the non-Western world. Although the formulation is rather broad, it is clear enough that the teaching of Trent on this matter was directed specifically against Martin Luther's effort to justify his friend and supporter, Philip of Hesse, who was not only a bigamist but also a very significant thorn in the side of the Roman Catholic Church at that time. In other words, Luther was being publicly attacked where he was very vulnerable indeed—where he was trying to hold a novel position which was contrary to both the established Christian practice and the common secular understanding of marriage in his own Western society. There were a few other ecclesiastical condemnations of polygyny, but these also must be understood and interpreted within the socio-historical context of Western Christendom.

Because the teaching of Trent was taken at face value and understood in a universally literal sense, the Roman Catholic position on polygyny was not even reconsidered as a result of the later missionary encounters with polygynous societies. Some of the other Christian Churches did actually debate the matter with reference to the widespread practice of polygyny met by their missionaries, especially in Africa.[19] But in general, or with very few exceptions, all Christian missionaries have maintained the absolute necessity of monogamy in accordance with the traditional practice of the Church in Europe. The tendency has been, almost everywhere, to identify the practice of monogamy with the New Testament *kerygma*. The previous acceptance of monogamy in practice has thus become for polygynists a condition, *sine qua non*, for the full acceptance of the Christian faith, even though the New Testament itself contains no explicit

---

[18] Cf. Denzinger, *Enchiridion Symbolorum*, nn. 465, 969, 972, 2231.
[19] Cf. L. Harries, "Christian Marriage in African Society," in *Survey of African Marriage and Family Life,* edited by Arthur Phillips (London, 1953), pp. 328ff.

identification of the Gospel leaven with an immediate and practical prohibition against polygyny.

Therefore, in the course of almost 2,000 years, Christian theologians have given very little attention to this problem of polygyny as a social institution. For them it was never a widespread and urgent problem. They encountered it only in individual cases which were seen as unusual deviations from the common and traditional pattern of social behavior in the Western world. The major encounters between Christianity and polygynous societies have occurred, for the most part, only more or less during the past one hundred years. And it is well known that very few of the missionaries sent out from the Western world during this time even attempted to understand the significance and the value of non-Western social institutions. The missionaries in general, like the theologians, simply took for granted that the prevailing social institutions of their own respective societies represented the most appropriate of human practices. These were uncritically regarded as properly Christian institutions; thus missionary activity was very much a matter of transplanting European institutions throughout the non-Western world, while generally ignoring or condemning the indigenous "pagan" social structures. Of course, it is not only missionaries and theologians who are ethnocentric in their approach to the *oikumene*.

Through a kind of universal culture-blindness, each people tends to regard its own social system and cultural pattern as normative for humanity. Given the opportunity, theologians have usually succeeded in bringing about a reconciliation between Christianity and the prevailing institutions of their own respective societies, and they have often enough managed to convince themselves and their contemporaries that even the most dubious of social practices are perfectly compatible with Christianity. A classical example of this is the socio-economic institution of slavery which was accepted and practiced among Christian peoples for centuries. This was eloquently "justified" by the most eminent churchmen and theologians, including St. Augustine and St. Thomas Aquinas.[20]

Now in the light of the modern social sciences, and with the decline of Western ethnocentrism in this post-colonial era, it is possible to attain a deeper appreciation of the significance and the value of non-Western social institutions and cultural forms. It should also be possible for Christian theologians to address themselves anew to such questions as the possible compatibility of Christianity with simultaneous polygyny under certain circumstances. At any rate—*and this is all that is being suggested here*—it might be found possible to tolerate the continuation of previously contracted polygynous marriages among people who, in certain concrete and limited social conditions, wish subsequently to become Christians.

A general principle, which might be used as a guide and a justification for some further theological investigation along these lines, is contained in Vatican Council II's *Decree on the Church's Missionary Activity:* "If, in certain regions, groups of men are found who are prevented from embracing the Catholic faith because they cannot adapt to a particular form which the Church has taken on there, it is desired that this circumstance be provided for in some special way, until such time as all the Christians concerned can gather together in one community" (n. 20).

Another principle, which might provide some guidance, is this: "Do not regard it as your task, and do not bring any pressure to bear on the peoples, to change their manners, customs and uses, unless they are evidently contrary to religion and sound morals. . . . There is no stronger cause for alienation and hate than an attack on local customs, especially when these go back to venerable antiquity. This is more especially the case when an attempt is made to introduce the customs of another people in place of those which have been abolished" ("Instruc-

[20] Cf. St. Augustine, *The City of God,* Bk. XIX, Ch. 15; St. Thomas Aquinas, *Summa Theologiae,* IIa-IIae, q. 57, a 3 & 4; q. 65, a 2.

tion to Missionaries in 1659," *Collect. Prop. Fide.*, 1907, Vol. I, p. 42).

Biblical and Theological Aspects

"The teaching of Jesus on marriage," according to J. L. McKenzie, "is limited to his affirmations on indissolubility." [21] Polygyny was not treated directly and explicitly by the New Testament writers who quite naturally, under the influence of the socio-ethical ethos of their particular time and place in history, accepted monogamy as the obvious and normal point of departure for any discussion of marriage.[22] The texts which are usually cited to show the incompatibility of Christianity and polygyny are concerned specifically with other matters.[23] This will be seen just by rereading them, while keeping in mind the exact notion of simultaneous polygyny.

Adultery, divorce, consecutive polygyny and polyandry are manifestly repudiated in the New Testament (cf. Mt. 5, 32; 19, 3–9; Mk. 10, 2–12; Rom. 7, 2–3; 1 Cor. 7, 2ff.; Eph. 5, 21–33). But simultaneous polygyny is not considered at all. All of the positive values urged in these texts—love, faithfulness, mutual respect for conjugal rights, and indissolubility—are also capable of realization within a system of simultaneous polygyny, without at the same time denying that they may be more fully realized in a monogamous union. The point here is that while the New Testament repudiates any number of practices (including prostitution and homosexuality) which compromise the Christian ideal of marriage, there is no mention of simultaneous polygyny—aside perhaps from the Pauline requirement that an official servant of the Church should be the husband of one wife only (1 Tim. 3, 2. 12; Tit. 1, 6). As Schillebeeckx points

---

[21] J. McKenzie, *op. cit.*, pp. 550f.

[22] Cf. E. Schillebeeckx, *op. cit.* I, p. 284.

[23] Cf. K. Barth, *Church Dogmatics* III-4 (Edinburgh, 1957), p. 199: "We can hardly point with certainty to a single text [of the New Testament] in which polygamy is expressly forbidden and monogamy universally decreed. If, then, we approach the Bible legalistically, we cannot honestly conclude that in this matter we are dealing with an unconditional law of God."

out, the New Testament contains no explicit commandment either in favor of monogamy or against polygyny.[24]

Thus the "divine positive law" forbidding a Christian to have more than one wife at the same time is something that has been deduced from Scripture by theologians, as a result of their interpretations and speculations, inside the boundaries of ancient Christendom. While affirming and defending the Christian ideal of monogamy, it appears that these theologians, perhaps overly influenced by their own Western tradition, have deduced more than is warranted by their biblical premises. It is significant that their traditional scriptural interpretation on this subject is invariably buttressed with arguments from reason and appeals to the natural law.[25]

Following Augustine and Aquinas, it is widely held that polygyny is not in itself evil, since it was clearly permitted by God according to the Old Testament revelation, and since it also conforms with the natural purpose of procreation. The rational argument against polygyny arises from its alleged incompatibility with "the secondary ends" of marriage, "inasmuch as it hinders domestic peace and reduces each of the wives to a condition of too great inferiority, and indirectly tends also to prejudice the child's education".[26] Such a generalization is a good example of culture-bound moralizing; it is meaningless except in relation to concrete sociological situations where it may, or may not, be verified in this or that actual case of polygyny within a particular historico-cultural and socio-economic context; it is not, as a matter of fact, universally true in the *real* world. This very same kind of moralizing could, of course, also be turned against monogamy, since in some cases of monogamy "the primary end" of marriage cannot be actually achieved, and adultery or divorce may follow.

[24] E. Schillebeeckx, *op. cit.* I, p. 284.

[25] See, for example, L. Ott, *Fundamentals of Catholic Dogma* (St. Louis, ⁴1960), p. 463: "Speculatively, the rectitude of monogamy is established by this, in that it alone guarantees the fulfilling of all the purposes of marriage. . . ."

[26] Buscaran and Ellis, *Canon Law Text and Commentary* (Milwaukee, 1964), pp. 400f.

It is usually affirmed uncritically that the sacramental symbolism of Christian marriage, based on the relationship of unifying love between Christ and the Church, can be realized only in a monogamous union. But one could argue, if one had a serious reason for doing so, that the "two in one flesh" unity, and therefore the sacramental significance, can also be realized in a polygynous marriage. This could be said in the same way that, for example, the several children of one mother may be regarded as "one flesh" with her by reason of their unity in generation and in maternal love. Such unity is not exclusive. The relationship between the mother and each child respectively may even be regarded as a union of "two in one flesh" without thereby excluding the other children from this same relationship with their mother. Therefore, by reason of a socially valid polygynous marriage, a man may be conjugally united with each of his wives respectively as "two in one flesh", since each wife does become with him "one flesh", and this kind of unity is not in itself exclusive by its very nature.

The Lord's reference to this unity of "flesh" in "the beginning" (Mt. 19, 4–6; Gen. 2, 22–24) need not be taken as a repudiation of polygyny. He was directly answering a question concerning divorce only, and the narrative to which he referred in connection with "two" becoming "one flesh" is not at all concerned with legal marriage custom, but with the origin of man and woman in relation to their mutual completion in one another on the basis of an indissoluble bond. "One flesh" means family unity, including also the relationships of the extended family unit. Such is the clear meaning of this word "flesh" in many other places (cf. Gen. 29, 14; 37, 27; Jgs. 9, 2; 2 Sam. 5, 1; 19, 12–13; 1 Chr. 11, 1).

It is also clear that the Lord's reference to "hardness of hearts" (Mt. 19, 8) concerns only the previous toleration of divorce. Even his use of the word "wife" in the singular does not necessarily exclude polygyny. In the marriage laws of Moses, which the Lord is discussing explicitly in this context, the same singular is used regularly with reference to marriage cases which may be either polygynous or monogamous (cf. Dt. 22, 13. 22; 24, 1).

Thus the union between Christ and the Church can also be symbolized in a simultaneously polygynous marriage. Christ, standing as the husband, is one, and the Church, as his spouse, is plural. The People of God is a plurality of persons united to Christ, although, in this relationship, they may also be regarded as one corporate person. The Old Testament, which recognized the validity of both polygynous and monogamous marriages (often without making any distinction between them), provided the groundwork for the New Testament notion and image of sacramental marriage.[27] The sacramental symbolism is originally based on the covenant union of Yahweh's love for the people of Israel who are many different persons, yet "one body", "one flesh", one family.

Ecclesiological Aspects

In other matters of long-standing Christian moral practice, radical changes and even reversals have taken place in the course of history. Thus it may be that the traditional attitude on this question of polygyny is not entirely irrevocable. The history of the Church's attitudes and practices, with regard to such socio-economic institutions as usury and slavery, is highly instructive. The following historical observations suggest some enlightening parallels with the problem under consideration here.

Usury—understood as any and every form of gaining profit on a loan—was clearly, forcefully, absolutely, comprehensively and repeatedly condemned and prohibited by three general councils of the Roman Catholic Church, and by numerous popes, bishops and theologians, following the common patristic teaching that all forms and practices of usury are explicitly regarded as sinful in both the Old and the New Testaments.[28] The Old Testament, in sharp contrast to its attitude toward polygyny, is

[27] Cf. J. McKenzie, op. cit., p. 550; L. Bouyer, Dictionary of Theology (New York, 1965), p. 292.
[28] Cf. J. Noonan, Jr., "Usury and Contraception," in Theology Digest, Vol. XV, No. 2, Summer 1967, pp. 105ff.

uncompromisingly opposed to usury. Even the New Testament, while silent about polygyny, explicitly repudiates usury in the Lord's own words: "Lend, expect nothing in return" (Lk. 6, 35).

But this particular teaching of the Church, which was based literally on the words of Scripture, and could therefore be regarded as "divine positive law", came under the scrutiny of later theologians. The prohibition was reconsidered by ecclesiastical authorities and eventually revoked. The decisive factor in bringing about a new moral attitude toward usury was the changing sociological conditions in 16th-century Europe. More and more, usury came to be recognized as a positive, constructive and integrated socio-economic institution in the societies of the Western world. The initial judgment of the Church had been inspired, made and framed in response to particular social dangers in previous, and no longer existing, social conditions.[29] Thus the Church's moral judgment was subsequently realigned with reference to the *really different* socio-economic conditions under which *other men* were living. The principle involved, as enunciated by Noonan, is this: "Specific moral rules enacted by the Church may be taken as sure guides for the times (and places) for which they are enacted, but they are not beyond reexamination and revision to preserve their purpose and to protect the permanent goods they safeguard. If the concrete circumstances of a society change (or if they differ radically in different societies), the requirements of justice and charity will change (or they will be concretely different in different societies)." [30]

For many centuries the socio-economic institution of slavery was regarded by the Church as quite compatible with the Christian life and conscience. St. Augustine taught that slavery was "a punishment for sin . . . and this is why the apostle (Eph. 4, 5) admonished slaves to be subject to their masters".[31] While economic forces within Christendom were gradually

---

[29] *Ibid.:* "The usury rule was a good rule for the economy of medieval village society. But this working rule, designed in the form of an absolute prohibition, was not to be confused with the unchanging moral law."

[30] *Ibid.* (Words in parentheses are added.)

[31] Cf. footnote 20.

transmuting slavery into serfdom, St. Thomas Aquinas cooly affirmed that "slavery among men is natural" and that "between masters and slaves there is a special right of domination", including the master's right to beat his slave.[32] Therefore, this socio-economic institution was "justified" by scriptural interpretation, and by a "natural law" rationale which can no longer be taken seriously.

The practice of simultaneous polygyny, as it may be observed today in many societies, could hardly be regarded as more incompatible with Christianity than was the institution of slavery. Yet slave owners were welcomed into the sacramental life of the Christian community without being first required to liberate their dubious socio-economic investments, while polygynists have never been, and still are not, accepted into the Church without first being required to cancel the socially valid and just contracts previously made by them with other persons.

Could it be that in particular times and places there are some deeply rooted socio-economic institutions which Christianity cannot change (and perhaps should not even try to change) immediately, even by outside legislation? Such things may, however, be transformed gradually from the inside by Christians who are supposed to function after the manner of a leaven within their own respective societies. Undoubtedly, this Christian leaven in the Western world had something to do with the gradual realization of the fact that Christianity and slavery are incompatible. Paul, Augustine and Aquinas were unable to see the full implications of their own belief that, on account of Christ, "there are no more distinctions . . . between slave and free" (Gal. 3, 28). But it is expected that the ideal of monogamy should be put into practice immediately among those who are just now, for the first time, turning to the Lord in faith.

Christian apologists have repeatedly taught, with special reference to slavery, that "the Church did not begin by condemning an institution which she found established, and which as a system of social and economic organization seemed then

[32] Ibid.

quite natural, if not necessary, to almost all the world. . . . Together with a *de facto* acceptance of the existing social regime there was brought into being a moral system which undermined its basis".[33] Why should not this very same approach be used in polygynous societies, where the moral leaven of Christianity can also be fully activated only through the participation of men in the sacramental life of the Church?

Objections Considered

It might be objected that the adoption of such an approach to the problem of polygyny would cause scandal within the existing Christian communities, and that it would tend to weaken Church discipline with regard to the ideal of monogamy.

The fact that some men who are already Christians, and who might have desires for more than one wife, might be scandalized by the toleration of polygyny among some new Christians; however, this is not in itself a sufficient reason for withholding the sacraments from the newly evangelized people in the case under discussion. Such scandal need not be avoided, as it would generally be only "pharisaic scandal". Even the less likely danger of "scandal of the weak" would be tolerable in this case by reason of the principle of double effect with reference to the good purpose of the sacraments.[34] The need that others have for the sacraments must take priority over the danger of scandal, because participation in the sacraments is a *necessary means* of salvation for all who have been truly evangelized.

After fourteen years of following the very policy suggested in this article, the Lutheran Church of Liberia has found "no indication that the Church's teaching on monogamy as the standard of Christian marriage is compromised by the practice of baptizing those who had previously entered into polygamy".[35] Thus the Lutheran Church in Liberia "stands firm in its convic-

[33] Cf. J. Zeiller, in *The History of the Primitive Church* I, by J. Lebreton and J. Zeiller (New York, 1944), p. 510.
[34] Cf. K. Rahner and H. Vorgrimler, *Theological Dictionary* (New York & London, 1965), p. 426.
[35] G. Currens and R. Payne, *op. cit.*, p. 3.

tion that it has been right in its policy of admitting polygamists into full membership in the Christian fellowship".[36]

The evaluation survey conducted by this Church indicates, moreover, that "the real problem with respect to the monogamous Christian is not his entering subsequently into a polygamous marriage, but rather the commiting of adultery".[37] Nor was this Lutheran community "inundated with polygamists". Since the number of polygamous marriages is "gradually decreasing, due to the pressure of economic and other social changes, it is unlikely that the proportion of polygamous to monogamous Christians will increase appreciably".[38]

Conclusion

The above considerations suggest the possibility of at least tolerating the continuation of previously contracted polygynous marriages among people who are subsequently evangelized in a society where polygyny is the prevailing cultural ideal, and socially integrated system, of marriage. A law which comes afterward does not necessarily annul a covenant previously ratified in good faith and without sin before God and men (cf. Gal.

[36] *Ibid.* Karl Barth, who also defends the ideal of monogamy, would surely agree with this policy; he says (*op. cit.,* p. 203): "Situations can and do actually arise in which the immediate abolition of polygamy as an institution (for example, the discharge of all but one of a man's existing wives) would bring about not only a cruel but an ethically irresponsible confusion and dissolution of social relationships which may be highly problematical, yet are not senseless and wicked, but are the guarantees of law and order and security and protection, and can no longer be so if there is an abrupt transition to monogamy. Situations can and do arise, therefore, in which it would be sheer brutality for the Christian Church to confront men with the choice between baptism and institutional polygamy. The decision of theological ethics in favor of monogamy as against polygamy calls for a clear recognition of matter and purpose. . . . There are exceptions. And they will always be worked out in accordance with a wise assessment of the situation."

[37] G. Currens and R. Payne, *op. cit.,* p. 2. In this connection, Barth also observes (*op. cit.,* p. 203) that "the institution of monogamy offers not the slightest guarantee . . . that the divine command of monogamy . . . will be kept and not transgressed". The Church is to proclaim the Christian ideal, not to *enforce* it and insist on its consequences even before people have come into the Church.

[38] G. Currens and R. Payne, *op. cit.,* p. 2.

3, 17). It might be possible, therefore, to tolerate such a practice in areas which—precisely because of the prevailing attitude toward polygyny—have so far remained impervious to the Christian message, and where it has been found impossible otherwise to introduce the leaven of Christianity.

Since this leaven can be properly effective among a people only through their active participation in the sacramental life of the Church, it would seem to be theologically unsound simply to evangelize such peoples and then prevent them from actually participating in this sacramental life. Such a compromise method might amount to putting people in bad faith, for the insistence on law can nullify the grace of God (cf. Gal. 2, 21). In any case, such a half-way missionary approach would not be conducive to the firm and indigenous establishment of the Church among the people.

Finally, this proposal for a full reconsideration of the traditional Christian approach to polygyny "takes into account, with all seriousness, the present condition of men who have not known the Good News, and of a society whose structures have not been influenced by Christian teaching".[39] Rather than imposing legalistically upon such men "a part of the Christian ethic retrospectively", it would seem more reasonable—and certainly more in conformity with the meaning and the primacy of faith and hope and love—to first bring them within the sphere of the Church's sacramental life of grace, and *then* to look for the gradual inner transformation of men and their respective social institutions.[40]

[39] *Ibid.*, p. 4.
[40] *Ibid.*

BIOGRAPHICAL NOTES

HEINRICH SCHLIER: Born in Germany in 1900, he studied at the universities of Leipzig and Marburg. He received his doctorate in theology in 1945 and is now honorary professor at the University of Bonn. His translated works include *Principalities and Powers in the New Testament* (in the Quaestiones Disputatae series). His new book, *The Relevance of the New Testament,* will be published in 1968.

KARL RAHNER, S.J.: Born in Germany in 1904, he was ordained in 1932. He studied at the universities of Freiburg im Breisgau and Innsbruck, receiving his doctorate in theology in 1936. He was formerly professor of the philosophy of religion and Christian anthropology at Munich University, and at present is professor of dogmatic theology and the history of dogma at the University of Münster. Among his many important works are *Schriften zur Theologie* (tr.: *Theological Investigations*) in seven volumes (1954-1966). He is also editor of the ten-volume *Lexikon für Theologie und Kirche* (1957-1965) and *Handbuch der Pastoraltheologie,* Vols. I-II (1964-1966).

OSMUND SCHREUDER, O.F.M.: Born in the Netherlands in 1925, he was ordained in 1958. He studied at the universities of Nijmegen and Frankfurt, receiving his doctorate in sociology in 1962. At present he is professor of religious and pastoral sociology at the University of Nijmegen. He has published several works on sociology in German and Dutch.

YVES CONGAR, O.P.: Born in France in 1904, he was ordained in 1930. He pursued his philosophical studies at the Institut Catholique in Paris and studied theology at Le Saulchoir in Etiolles, France. From 1931 to 1954 he was professor of fundamental theology and ecclesiology at Le Saulchoir. His published works include *Lay People in the Church* (1957), *After Nine Hundred Years* (1959), *Laity, Church and World* (1960), *The Mystery of the Church* (1960), *The Mystery of the Temple* (1962), and *The Meaning of Tradition* (1964).

FRANZ BÖCKLE: Born in Switzerland, in 1921, he was ordained in 1945. He studied at the Angelicum in Rome and at the University of Munich, earning his doctorate in theology in 1952. He has been a professor of moral theology in the seminary in Chur, Switzerland, and is at present professor at the University of Bonn. His published works deal with general ethical and moral problems.

HELMUT GOLLWITZER: A member of the Lutheran Church, he was born in Germany in 1908. He studied philosophy and theology at various universities in Germany, receiving his doctorate in theology in 1937. At present he lectures in systematic theology at the Free University of Berlin. Among his published works are *Denken und Glauben* (1965) and *Von der Stellvertretung Gottes* (1967).

DOMINGO CASTAGNA: Born in Argentina in 1931, he was ordained in 1955. He studied at the University of the Lateran in Rome and at the Lumen Vitae Center in Brussels, receiving a "Peritus in re pastorali" diploma in 1964. He is presently in charge of the pastoral theology course at the Catholic University of Salvador.

LEO WALTERMANN: Born in Germany in 1928, he is currently director of the Religious Broadcasting Service of the German Radio, and has edited two series of reports for West German radio on *The Council as a Trial* and *The Clergy between Science and the Pastoral Ministry*.

KARL LEHMANN: Born in Germany in 1926, he was ordained in 1963. He studied at the University of Freiburg im Breisgau in Germany and at the Gregorian in Rome, receiving his doctorate in philosophy in 1962. He is an associate of Karl Rahner at the University of Munich and collaborates on *Lexikon für Theologie und Kirche* and *Handbuch der Pastoraltheologie*.

LUIS MALDONADO: Born in Spain, he was ordained in 1954. He studied at the universities of Comillas and Salamanca in Spain, and at the universities of Innsbruck, Austria and Freiburg im Breisgau in Germany, gaining his degree in philosophy and a doctorate in theology. Since 1962 he has been professor of liturgy at the Institute of Pastoral Studies at the University of Salamanca. His publications include *La plegaría eucarística* (1967) and *El Mensaje de los Christianos* (1965).

DOMENICO GRASSO, S.J.: Born in Italy in 1917, he was ordained in 1947. He studied at the University of Naples and at the Gregorian in Rome, receiving a doctorate in theology. Presently a professor of pastoral theology at the Gregorian, he is the author of two books on preaching published in Italy and has contributed to several reviews, among them *Gregorianum* and *Civiltà Cattolica*.

FRANÇOIS COUDREAU: Born in France in 1916, he was ordained in 1943. He studied at the Institut Catholique in Paris and founded the Institut Supérieur de Pastorale Catéchétique, also in Paris, of which he is still the honorary director. He is a parish priest in a Paris suburb and also serves as general treasurer of the Bureau Internationale Catholique de l'Enfance in Rome. His published works include *Le Catéchuménat des adultes* (1960) and *Une pastorale qui s'interroge* (1964).

MICHAEL FRICKEL, O.S.B.: Born in Germany in 1921, he was ordained in 1951. He studied at the Athenaeum of St. Anselm in Rome, receiving his doctorate in theology in 1956. He is secretary of the German Association of Catholic Preachers and the editor of *Sprache und Predigt* (1963).

HERMAN BORGERT, C.SS.R.: Born in 1912 in the Netherlands, he was ordained in 1938. He studied at the University of Nijmegen and at the Institut Catholique in Paris, receiving his doctorate in theology in 1959. A professor of pastoral theology at the Redemptorist Studium in Wittem, he is the author of *Theologie en Prediking* (1956) and *Kerk in toekomst pleidooi voor een meer wereldse kerk* (1966).

JÓZEF MAJKA: Born in Poland in 1918, he was ordained in 1942. He studied in Poland at the major seminary of Tarnow, at the University of Cracow and at the Catholic University of Lublin, receiving advanced degrees in theology and the social sciences and a doctorate in philosophy. He lectures at the Catholic University of Lublin and is editor of the review *Roczniki Filozoficzne*.

FRANÇOIS LEPARGNEUR, O.P.: Born in France in 1925, he was ordained in 1955. He studied at the universities of Caen and Paris and at Cornell University in New York, receiving a degree in theology and a doctorate in law. At present he lectures in ecclesiology at the Dominican House of Studies in Brazil, where he has been stationed since 1959. He is also the co-author of a work on the problems of priests in Brazil, published in 1965.

JUAN OCHAGAVÍA, S.J.: Born in Chile in 1928, he was ordained in 1957. After studies at Woodstock College, Maryland, and the University of Munich, he received his doctorate in theology in 1962. He teaches dogmatic theology at the Catholic University of Santiago and is assistant editor of the review *Mensaje*.

DANIEL MORRISEY, O.P.: Born in Wisconsin in 1936, he was ordained in 1962. He studied at the Aquinas Institute of Theology in the United States, and in Paris at the Institut Pastorale Catéchétique and the Institut Catholique, receiving an advanced degree in theology and a doctorate in philosophy. With Karl Rahner he is editor of a new series of pastoral studies, of which the first volume, *The Theology of Pastoral Action*, will be published in 1968.

HEINZ SCHUSTER: Born in Germany in 1930, he was ordained in 1955. He studied at the universities of Innsbruck and Trêves, receiving his doctorate in theology in 1962. Two of his studies appear in the *Handbuch der Pastoraltheologie*. He is on the editorial board of *Diakonia* and contributes to *Lexikon für Theologie und Kirche*.

KARLHEINZ HOFFMANN, S.J.: Born in Germany in 1927, he was ordained in 1959. He holds degrees in philosophy and theology and works at the German Catholic Television Center. The author of various essays, he is presently engaged in a study of the effects of religious broadcasts.

EUGENE HILLMAN, C.S.SP.: Born in Boston in 1924, he was ordained in 1950. After receiving a degree in theology, he has since 1952 been working as a missionary among the Masai tribe in North Tanzania. Among his works are *The Church as Mission* (1965). His new book, *The Wider Ecumenism*, will be published in 1968.

International Publishers of CONCILIUM

ENGLISH EDITION
Paulist Press
Glen Rock, N. J., U.S.A.

Burns & Oates Ltd.
25 Ashley Place
London, S.W.1

DUTCH EDITION
Uitgeverij Paul Brand, N. V.
Hilversum, Netherlands

FRENCH EDITION
Maison Mame
Tours/Paris, France

JAPANESE EDITION (PARTIAL)
Nansôsha
Tokyo, Japan

GERMAN EDITION
Verlagsanstalt Benziger & Co., A.G.
Einsiedeln, Switzerland

Matthias Grunewald-Verlag
Mainz, W. Germany

SPANISH EDITION
Ediciones Guadarrama
Madrid, Spain

PORTUGUESE EDITION
Livraria Morais Editora, Ltda.
Lisbon, Portugal

ITALIAN EDITION
Editrice Queriniana
Brescia, Italy